Your Daily RESET

Daily Inspiration and Motivation for Living Your Life of Purpose with Passion

Dr. Jason Brooks

Your Daily RESET

© 2014 by Dr. Jason Brooks

All rights reserved. No portion of this book may be reproduced, stored in a retrieval system, or transmitted in any form or by any means – electronic, mechanical, photocopy, recording, or other – except for brief quotations in critical reviews or articles, without the prior written permission of the publisher.

All quotations used in this book were researched for appropriate attribution to the original author. Any missed or incorrect attributions are unintentional. Corrections to the attributions should be sent to info@danapublishing.com and will be corrected.

Published by DANA Publishing

Unless otherwise noted, Scripture quotations are taken from the Holy Bible, New International Version, retrieved from www.YouVersion.com

978-0-9909893-0-1
978-0-9909893-1-8 (hardcover)

Brooks, Jason, 1969-
Your Daily RESET/by Dr. Jason Brooks
ISBN 978-0-9909893-0-1

For Darla, Andrew, Nathanael, and Aleya. I pray you always find inspiration and love in every moment.

Thanks to...

My mentors who have motivated and inspired me through the years. Though we may never have met, you have left a lasting mark on my life.

The outstanding team at Addiction Campuses. You give so much of yourselves every day to bring hope and freedom from addiction and foster mental health wellness for all clients you serve. You are making a difference in the lives of many.

Higher Level Management. Thanks for your support and expertise in bringing outstanding Christian events to the stage and for your passion for sharing the message of the gospel.

Trevor, Tracy, and Falon Mansfield. You stood by our family and supported us during the tough times. I love you and thank God for you. I'm so blessed you are part of my life.

Bryan, Barb, Austin, Alex, and Brandon White. Your love and support during the difficult times in my life has been an incredible blessing. God has used you to show the real meaning of sacrificial love.

Stephen, Beth, Emma, and Ethan Brooks. Thanks for your prayers and support as I have pursued God's call on my life. You are amazing and I appreciate you more than you know.

Theresa and Darwin White. Over twenty years ago you opened your hearts and welcomed me into your family as your son when I promised to love, honor, and cherish your daughter...for better or for worse...the rest of our lives. Thank you for your encouragement and support to help me live my dreams.

Tom and Alice Brooks, my parents. Your unending support of me, during the twists and turns of life, is truly amazing. You have always stood by me, regardless of where the road led, and have been my greatest cheerleaders. I love you both.

Andrew, Nathanael, and Aleya. I love you more than you can imagine. I am so proud of each of you and honored to be your Dad. God has a special purpose and plan for each of you and I look forward to celebrating the incredible journey He has in store.

My bride, Darla. You are my light and my inspiration. Through the good times and bad, we've held tight to each other. I'm so glad we're on this amazing adventure together and I look forward to seeing how God is leading us together to touch lives...one step at a time.

My Heavenly Father and Savior, Jesus Christ. Over the years, You have taken me through some wonderful times and others so challenging I didn't know if I could make it through. But through every season, I knew I was never alone. You walked with me each step of the way and I know each day You are masterfully making me into the man You created me to be. Thank You for the blessings of my life and for each opportunity I have to pour into the lives of others by bringing hope, healing, growth and inspiration to everyone I meet. I love You and trust You with all I am for your glory!

A Welcome Message from Dr. Jason

Hope...healing...inspiration...change...growth...success! These words are the desire of most of us but found by very few. We often trudge through our days just going through the motions, missing the energy and enthusiasm that comes from living a life of purpose with passion. I see it in the eyes of people I meet every day. Behind the gratuitous smiles are pains of the past, struggles of the present, and uncertainty for the future.

In my first book, *RESET: Reformatting Your Purpose for Tomorrow's World*, I helped folks create a vivid picture of a life and legacy they wanted to leave and build a life of success. I outlined a step by step process to follow ultimately resulting in creating life balance and wellness and establishing a clear sense of life direction by identifying life purpose, unleashing your passion, establishing plans to accomplish your goals, developing strategies to overcome obstacles when they arise, and living a life of praise, giving thanks for the successes achieved. The response to *RESET* was overwhelming as readers were able to apply the ideas, principles, and personal exploration to their lives, push the reset button, and begin for the first time living with intentionality and focus.

For many, this was the first step of a commitment to a life of RESET. With any commitment, discipline, and encouragement is important to stay on track. It is with this in mind that I proudly present *Your Daily RESET*. We all need someone to walk with us on our journey... to provide inspiration during the days where the obstacles to stay on track are great and to celebrate the progress we're making each and every moment.

I'm an encourager, healer, and teacher at heart. Your Daily RESET is a labor of love for me...love for each of you who have committed to resisting the voice to live a life of mediocrity and desiring something greater for yourself...the life God created for you to live.

I wrote *Your Daily RESET* with you on my mind and on my heart. It's designed to provide daily inspiration for you through motivational quotes by some of the greatest inspirational writers, visionary leaders, and legacy creators in history. Also, included each day are thought provoking questions related to the inspirational message to guide you through personal self-exploration and discovery, healing from the past, focus on the present, and help you to create a life of gratitude and success for the future. As you grow, the questions will continue to challenge and inspire you, year after year, to move deeper into discovering the masterpiece you were created to be and allow God to speak to your heart.

In a world where we're often overwhelmed with difficulties and challenges, it's important to be intentional with our thoughts and commit time to giving praise and gratitude for who we are and the lives we live. My heart's desire is to come along side you to support on your journey to live the life you've always imagined...a life of purpose with passion! Don't be like everyone else! Don't accept average as the norm. Embrace your place and live the life you were created to live to the fullest. You have a story to tell and a song to sing. Each day is an opportunity for a brand new start...a RESET! This is your daily reset!

Live your life of purpose with passion!
Dr. Jason

Your Daily RESET

Daily Inspiration and Motivation for Living Your Life of Purpose with Passion

Day 1

"Winners are not those who never fail but those who never quit."

~ Edwin Louis Cole

Your Daily RESET!

What's something you are on the verge of quitting that you know you need to persevere through? God will equip you and give you the strength to keep going if you will only ask for His help.

Day 2

"The grass is greener where you water it."

~ Neil Barringham

Your Daily RESET!

How are you investing in yourself, your situation, your relationships, your health, and your development today? Are you watering your life or content to just let it wither and die?

Day 3

"If you do not change direction, you may end up where you are heading."

~ Lao Tzu

Your Daily RESET!

What direction are you headed in your life? We all eventually arrive at a destination...however, only very few arrive there on purpose. What type of person are you?

Day 4

"The greatest tragedy of life is not unanswered prayer, but unoffered prayer."

~ F. B. Meyer

Your Daily RESET!

What have you resisted praying for? What's held you back? Take time right now to pray...God is listening.

Day 5

"Respect people who find time for you in their busy schedule. But love people who never look at their schedule when you need them."

~ Author Unknown

Your Daily RESET!

Think about someone in your life who you know without a doubt would be there for you if you needed them. No questions asked. Give them a call today and thank them for their love and willingness to sacrifice for you.

Day 6

"Sometimes I have to remind myself that I don't have to do what everyone else is doing."

~ Author Unknown

Your Daily RESET!

In what areas have you settled and compromised because of the actions or expectations of others? What do you need to start doing different today to start being your authentic self?

Day 7

"The first to say sorry is the bravest. The first to forgive is the strongest. The first to forget is the happiest. Be the best - always be first!"

~ Author Unknown

Your Daily RESET!

How often are you the first one to say you're sorry? If this is not the norm for you, what holds you back from bringing an apology first? Three of the most powerful phrases in strong relationships are "I'm sorry…Thank you…and I love you". Make it a point to use these today.

Day 8

"Sometimes the bad things that happen in our lives put us directly on the path to the best things that will ever happen to us."

~ Nicole Reed

Your Daily RESET!

Think back on a time when something "bad" happened in your life only to find out later it opened the door to something even "better". What did you learn from the experience? Is there a "bad" situation you're facing today? What can you take from your past experience and apply to your situation today to help you make it through?

Day 9

"To be yourself in a world that is constantly trying to make you something else is the greatest accomplishment."

~ Ralph Waldo Emerson

Your Daily RESET!

How important is it for you to "fit in" to what others expect of you? How easy is it for you to resist the "status quo" and let your unique voice be heard and your light shine to touch the lives of others? Let your voice sing the song in your heart.

Day 10

"When it rains, look for rainbows. When it's dark, look for stars."

~ Unknown

Your Daily RESET!

What stars are shining in your life?

Day 11

"Worrying does not take away tomorrow's troubles, it takes away today's peace."

~ Author Unknown

Your Daily RESET!

What are you worried about today? Make a list of the top 5 things that are causing you to worry. Now, going one by one through the list, give thanks for the ability to grow stronger through each of these situations which are causing you worry.

Day 12

"It's the possibility of having a dream come true that makes life interesting."

~ Paulo Coelho

Your Daily RESET!

What are the dreams you're dreaming in your life? What intentional steps are you taking to help make these dreams a reality?

Day 13

"The road to success is not crowded. Because while most are looking for ways to take, the truly successful people are finding ways to give. With a giving attitude, every situation is an opportunity for success."

~ Author Unknown

Your Daily RESET!

How are you giving to others today? Look intentionally for opportunities to pour your time, talent, treasure, and talk into someone else's life and make a difference for them today.

Day 14

"Lack of direction, not lack of time, is the problem. We all have twenty-four hour days."

~ Zig Ziglar

Your Daily RESET!

Where are you going today? How are you being intentional with every moment of every day?

Day 15

"Be the kind of person that you want to meet."

~ Author Unknown

Your Daily RESET!

What are the characteristics of the type of person you want to meet and would enjoy spending time with? How many of those characteristics do you display? What changes do you need to make in yourself to attract the type of person you want to meet?

Day 16

"Twenty years from now you will be more disappointed by the things that you didn't do than by the ones you did do. So throw off the bowlines, sail away from safe harbor. Catch the trade winds in your sails. Explore. Dream. Discover."

~ H. Jackson Brown Jr.

Your Daily RESET!

What's holding you back today from moving forward and doing something you've always dreamed of doing? Make a list of those things. Now, review the list and place a line through the things that are just fears and have no real substance. Now, draw a line through those that are your personal insecurities. What's left on the list? Don't let anything stand in your way of doing what you dream of doing.

Day 17

"Never allow yourself to be so desperate that you end up settling for far less than what you deserve."

~ Author Unknown

Your Daily RESET!

Have you found in your life that during times of desperation, where you think things are coming apart at the seams, you end up settling for something "less than" rather than continuing to reach and strive for the best God has for you? What are you settling for today in your life? What has brought you to the point of needing to settle?

Day 18

"Each of us is on a unique journey in life. We have the chance to pursue our own purpose, our own passion, our own plans and live a life that is uniquely our own."

~ Dr. Jason Brooks

Your Daily RESET!

Do you have a clear vision of the story of your life? Can you see in your minds eye, through every season of life, all of the areas of your life? Your sense of self? The quality and depth of your relationships? Your spiritual growth? Your physical health and care? Your self-development? The satisfaction and impact of your work? Your monetary worth and your ability to give to others from your financial blessings?

Day 19

"People with goals succeed because they know where they are going...It's as simple as that."

~ Earl Nightingale

Your Daily RESET!

Do you know you were created for a purpose? You are not here by accident. Finding that purpose and intentionally pursuing it each and every day will bring the greatest success possible. Success is different for everyone. You will decide what success means to you aligned with your purpose, as God works His plans in your life.

Day 20

> "The greatest weapon against stress is our ability to choose one thought over another."
>
> ~ William James

Your Daily RESET!

What thoughts are you choosing in your life? Do you focus your thoughts more on hope, growth, and inspiration or on fear, decline, and defeat? What changes do you need to make in your thought life today?

Day 21

"The sign of a beautiful person is that they always see beauty in others."

~ Omar Suleiman

Your Daily RESET!

Take time today to look for the beauty in others. If you're really an overachiever…take a moment to tell the person what it is that makes them beautiful to you and what you appreciate in them.

Day 22

"If you want to change you have to be willing to be uncomfortable."

~ Author Unknown

Your Daily RESET!

Are you willing to make yourself uncomfortable in order to grow? What's holding you back from stretching yourself beyond what you ever thought possible?

Day 23

"No matter how hard it is, just keep going because you only fail when you give up."

~ Author Unknown

Your Daily RESET!

Think back on a time when you persevered through a difficult situation. What did you learn about yourself through that time which you can apply to your life today?

Day 24

"Knowing when to walk away is wisdom. Being able to is courage. Walking away, with your head held high, is dignity."

~ Author Unknown

Your Daily RESET!

Think about a time when you walked away from a difficult situation. Take time now to celebrate this decision and the wisdom, courage, and dignity you showed and experienced as a result of this situation.

Day 25

"Almost every successful person begins with two beliefs: the future can be better than the present, and I have the power to make it so."

~ David Brooks

Your Daily RESET!

What is your belief about your ability to create the future you desire for yourself? What's holding you back from taking the next steps to create that future?

Day 26

"Nothing soothes the soul quite like a walk on the beach."

~ Author Unknown

Your Daily RESET!

Think back to the last time you took a walk on the beach. What was the experience like for you? Can you still hear the sound of the surf, the smell of the salty-air, the sand under your feet, the sea breeze blowing on your face? There is something incredibly powerful and healing about the ocean. Commit now to taking a few minutes each week to meditate on the experience and give thanks for the times you've been able to take walks on the beach and soak in the power of the sea.

Day 27

"REST. It's part of the Program!"

~ Author Unknown

Your Daily RESET!

How important is rest in your life? Are you intentional with your times to recharge, refresh, and reset? Or, do you find that you're burning the candle at both ends and wearing yourself out. Rest is a biblical principle we often forget. God rested on the seventh day after creation. Jesus rested and set aside time for His disciples to rest from the work of ministry. Make plans now to set time aside this week to rest.

Day 28

"Start today to make the rest of your life the best of your life!"

~ Dr. Jason Brooks

Your Daily RESET!

What would "the best of your life" look like? What's holding you back from creating that incredible life for yourself? Fear, uncertainty, doubt...Don't let anything hold you back any longer.

Day 29

"The two most important days in your life are the day you are born, and the day you find out why."

~ Mark Twain

Your Daily RESET!

Do you know why you were born...the purpose of your life? Are you just going through the motions or are you living with intentionality, committing every moment to let the fullness of your purpose be revealed? How important is it for you to know your purpose?

Day 30

"Being challenged in life is inevitable. Being defeated is optional."

~ Roger Crawford

Your Daily RESET!

Think back on a time when you faced challenges and overcame those challenges. What did you learn from the experience?

Day 31

"Don't let your dreams be dreams."

~ Jack Johnson

Your Daily RESET!

What does it take to move dreams to reality? Action! What dreams have you held for years that just seem to be sitting still and going nowhere? Consider today one step you could take, just one, to get unstuck and start moving forward to bringing the dreams God has placed in your heart to reality.

Day 32

"He who is not courageous enough to take risks will accomplish nothing in life."

~ Muhammad Ali

Your Daily RESET!

What challenges are you facing today that require you to be courageous? How do you need to show courage today? Remember, you have everything you need right now to overcome the challenges you're facing today. The difference between success and failure is not in what you believe of yourself. It's in maintaining a mindset of confidence and courage.

Day 33

> "In three words, I can sum up everything I know about life: It goes on."
>
> ~ Robert Frost

Your Daily RESET!

Make a list of the advice and insight you would like to share with others from your life experiences? Pass it on.

Day 34

"Go forward in life with a twinkle in your eye and a smile on your face, but with great and strong purpose in your heart."

~ Gordon B. Hinckley

Your Daily RESET!

What is your life purpose? Do you have a strong sense of who you are and why you're here? Do you find joy in every moment knowing that you are here for a reason and you are making a difference in the lives of others?

Day 35

"A year from now you will wish you had started today."

~ Karen Lamb

Your Daily RESET!

Make a list of 5 things you've been meaning to start, but haven't. Choose one thing and start now. With this one action, you will start momentum to accomplish all five over the coming weeks and months.

Day 36

"Create a life that feels good on the inside, not one that just looks good on the outside."

~ Author Unknown

Your Daily RESET!

Is it more important for you to have a life that looks good to others or feels great to yourself? What kind of life are you creating?

Day 37

"Sometimes you have to let people go because they are toxic to you. Let them go because they take and take and leave you empty. Let them go because in the ocean of life, when all you're trying to do is stay afloat, they are the anchor that's drowning you."

~ Author Unknown

Your Daily RESET!

Do you have a toxic person, or people, in your life? What is one thing you can do different today to begin the process of removing those folks from your life?

Day 38

"Right now, therefore, every time we get the chance, let us work for the benefit of all."

Galatians 6:10, *The Holy Bible*

Your Daily RESET!

In what ways are you giving yourself for the benefit of others today? How are you investing your time, talent, talk, and treasure to make a difference in someone else's life?

Day 39

"Success will never be a big step in the future. Success is a small step taken just now."

~ Jonathan Martenssov

Your Daily RESET!

When you think of success, what comes to mind? Is it something big and grandiose or is success more about taking the next right step in your life and living your greatest potential today? We all need to take time to dream but never forget that success comes in the miracles of each moment.

Day 40

"Think continually in terms of the rewards of success rather than the penalties of failure."

~ Brian Tracy

Your Daily RESET!

Are you more of a "glass half empty" or "glass half full" type of person? Do you typically see the good or negative in situations and people? Often, experiencing happiness in life is built on perspective and making the choice to look for the good rather than the bad in every situation.

Day 41

"There will come a time when you believe everything is finished. That will be the beginning."

~ Louis L'Amour

Your Daily RESET!

Think back on a time when you thought "It's finished...I'm finished...There's nowhere else to turn." Remember, there's always another step to take and it's often the beginning of a brand new adventure.

Day 42

"Growth is painful. Change is painful. But nothing is as painful as staying stuck somewhere you don't belong."

~ Mandy Hale

Your Daily RESET!

Think back on a time when you went through a painful experience that you later saw as a time when you grew. What did you learn through that season which you can apply to your life today?

Day 43

"To accomplish great things, we must not only act, but also dream, not only plan, but also believe."

~ Anatole France

Your Daily RESET!

Think back on a time when you created plans to accomplish a goal you had set for yourself. Was it a challenge for you to create those plans? How important is planning for you today? Take time today to identify one goal and list the necessary steps to accomplish the goal.

Day 44

"Live out of your imagination, not your history."

~ Stephen R. Covey

Your Daily RESET!

Do you spend more focus remembering the past or looking to the future? Are you held captive to the pain you've experienced in years gone by or, through forgiveness, finding freedom to create a better life ahead? The choice is yours.

Day 45

"Embrace and love your body. It is the most amazing thing you will ever own."

~ Author Unknown

Your Daily RESET!

What are the thoughts that come to mind when you consider your body? What do you love about yourself? Take time now to celebrate the miracle and beauty of your physical body.

Day 46

"Worrying is a waste of time. It doesn't change anything. It messes with your mind and steals your happiness."

~ Author Unknown

Your Daily RESET!

How has worry held you back in the past? What can you do today to resist the "worry thief"?

Day 47

"Excuses are a time thief. Have a goal, accept responsibility, and take action."

~ Steve Maraboli

Your Daily RESET!

What excuses have you been using to keep you from moving forward with taking responsibility and action for your life? Make a commitment today to accept no excuses and press on.

Day 48

"Forget the day's troubles. Remember the day's blessings."

~ Prayer Quote

Your Daily RESET!

What are you thankful for today? Take time now to give thanks to God for the blessings in your life. He is the giver of all good things.

Day 49

"Everything you have in your life today you have attracted to yourself because of the person you are."

~ Brian Tracy

Your Daily RESET!

What have you attracted to yourself? What do you want to attract to yourself? Who do you need to become in order to attract what you desire?

Day 50

"The artist is nothing without the gift, but the gift is nothing without work."

~ Emile Zola

Your Daily RESET!

Did you know each of us has a purpose and has been given gifts to live our unique purpose? However, gifts without action often go unopened and unappreciated. How are you using your gifts today to touch others?

Day 51

"Be yourself. It's beautiful!"

~ Author Unknown

Your Daily RESET!

Take time now to make a list of the things you love about yourself. Give thanks for how God made you and know you are right were you are today for a reason. Every day you have the opportunity to become even more of the person God created you to be.

Day 52

"In all things, give thanks!"

I Thessalonians 5:19, *The Holy Bible*

Your Daily RESET!

How easy is it for you to give thanks in your life? Are you able to see things to be grateful for or do you have to search and search? Take time now to make a list of 10 things you are thankful for in your life.

Day 53

"Everything you do has the power to change the world. We never know who will be touched by our words, or inspired by our actions."

~ Author Unknown

Your Daily RESET!

Who has been an inspiration to you in the past? How have you inspired others? Remember, every encounter you have today has the potential to be an inspiration or devastation. The choice is yours.

Day 54

"Life is an opportunity, benefit from it. Life is beauty, admire it. Life is a dream, realize it. Life is a challenge, meet it. Life is a duty, complete it. Life is a game, play it. Life is a promise, fulfill it. Life is sorrow, overcome it. Life is a song, sing it."

~ Mother Teresa

Your Daily RESET!

Take time now to make a list of the words you would use to describe your life. When complete, review the list. What words do you like? Circle them. What words would you like to change? Place a line through them and write the word you would want it to be to the side of the first. What's one thing you could do differently today to start on the path to creating the life you desire?

Day 55

"Don't be upset by the results you didn't get with the work you didn't do."

~ Author Unknown

Your Daily RESET!

How are you giving of yourself to accomplish the goal you've identified? What are you willing to give to accomplish your dreams?

Day 56

> "The distance between what we are and what we want to be is a leap of faith. Make the jump!"
>
> ~ Dr. Jason Brooks

Your Daily RESET!

Think back to a time when you had to take a "leap of faith" in an area of your life. What was it like for you? What did you learn from the experience?

Day 57

"Do the best you can until you know better. Then, when you know better, do better."

~ Maya Angelou

Your Daily RESET!

What is one area of your life today you are struggling in? Do you feel like giving up? Don't give in…you are learning, you are growing, and someday soon you will figure it out. When that day comes, you will be so glad you didn't give up.

Day 58

"For one minute, walk outside, stand there, in silence, look up at the sky, and contemplate how amazing life is."

~ Author Unknown

Your Daily RESET!

This is a great exercise to do right now. To be completely present in the moment, mindful of every part of this experience, giving thanks for the life you have, and celebrating the gift of "the present".

Day 59

"Life is unpredictable and you never know what is coming next. Don't ever get too comfortable. Always be ready for change."

~ Author Unknown

Your Daily RESET!

Has your journey in life turned out the way you had expected? No matter where you're at in your life, chances are you have experienced something, or many things, that were not expected. We may not know what's ahead but God does. He's never surprised and He's walking with you every step of the way. Take His hand and celebrate the great adventure of life.

"Fear is a liar."

~ Author Unknown

Your Daily RESET!

Think back on a time when you resisted doing something because you were afraid. Fear tells you a situation will be worse than you imagine, you'll never win, and you'll always fail. In reality, failure only comes when we don't try. It takes just as much emotional energy to have fear as it does to have faith...both are evidences of things unseen.

Day 61

> "Success is stumbling from failure to failure with no loss of enthusiasm."
>
> ~ Winston Churchill

Your Daily RESET!

What does failure mean to you? How has failure been a stepping stone to success for you? How has failure in the past held you back from future success?

Day 62

"Follow your heart. Live your dream. Be passionate. Happiness is yours to take. Never give up. Your energy is limitless. Embrace possibility. Love your life."

~ Author Unknown

Your Daily RESET!

What are you passionate about? How is that passion driving you to live your purpose to the fullest?

Day 63

"If you don't make the time to work on creating the life you want, you're eventually going to be forced to spend a lot of time dealing with a life you don't want."

~ Kevin Ngo

Your Daily RESET!

Take time today to create a crystal clear picture of the life you want. Then, make a list of three things you can start doing differently that will help bring your vision into reality.

Day 64

> "People often say that motivation doesn't last. Well, neither does bathing. That's why we recommend it daily."
>
> ~ Zig Ziglar

Your Daily RESET!

What do you do to motivate yourself? What daily disciplines do you have that keep you fired up and excited for the opportunities ahead? If staying motivated is a challenge for you, what is one thing you could start doing today to begin turning the flywheel of inspiration and motivation.

Day 65

"A bad attitude is like a flat tire. You can't go anywhere until you change it."

~ Author Unknown

Your Daily RESET!

What's your attitude right now? Is it joyful or bitter? What are your expectations for the day? The reality is no matter what your expectations, they will most likely come true. So, why not expect the best and maintain a positive attitude?

Day 66

> "One step. That's all it takes. Start today. Whatever grand goal you have. Break inertia and take a single step...today."
>
> ~ Darren Hardy

Your Daily RESET!

What's one step you need to take today to move in the direction of living your dreams and accomplishing your goals?

Day 67

"Surround yourself with positive people."

~ Author Unknown

Your Daily RESET!

Make a list of the 10 most positive people in your life? Send them a message today to thank them for their inspiration and encouragement for you.

Day 68

"You are made to move. Yourself. And others."

~ Author Unknown

Your Daily RESET!

How are you inspiring others today? No matter where you are...no matter what you do...you have the chance to be a refreshing "drink of cold water" to someone in need. Look for an opportunity today to encourage someone and see what a difference it makes in your life.

Day 69

"We cannot become what we want to be by remaining what we are."

~ Max DePree

Your Daily RESET!

What steps do you need to take today on the journey to becoming who you want to be? What do you need to start doing? What do you need to stop doing? Now, do it!

Day 70

"Think Positive. Be Positive."

~ Author Unknown

Your Daily RESET!

Did you know thoughts have a huge influence who you are? If your thoughts are often of sadness, guilt, shame, and defeat, you will behave and live in that way. But, if your thoughts are often of joy, victory, freedom, and praise, you will live a life of happiness and abundance. Make the choice today to discipline your thoughts for the life you want to live.

Day 71

"One of the happiest moments ever is when you feel the courage to let go of what you can't change."

~ Author Unknown

Your Daily RESET!

What is a challenging situation you're facing today you know you cannot change? First, accept the reality you cannot change the situation. Next, make a list of the possible responses you could have to the situation. Finally, choose a response and take the first step in the direction. The reality is we cannot control the wind...but we can control the set of our sail.

Day 72

"Never underestimate your ability to make someone else's life better—even if you never know it."

~ Greg Louganis

Your Daily RESET!

Think back on a time when someone invested in your life and made a lasting impression on you. Take time today to reach out to that person and thank them for the investment they made in you.

Day 73

> "Rejection is God's way of saying 'wrong direction'."
>
> ~ Author Unknown

Your Daily RESET!

Think back on a time when you felt you were being rejected. What did you learn from the experience?

Day 74

"Isn't it funny how day by day nothing changes but when you look back everything is different..."

~ C.S. Lewis

Your Daily RESET!

Think about a time when you thought you were stuck and unable to move, but in hindsight realized even through the experience, you were growing.

Day 75

"Your time is limited, so don't waste it living someone else's life."

~ Steve Jobs

Your Daily RESET!

How much control do other people have of your life? Your thoughts? Your feelings? Your time? Are you willingly giving this control out of a heart of service or is it being stolen from you because of fear of confrontation or other false beliefs that lead you to give control of your life to other people? What should you be doing different?

Day 76

"It will hurt. It will take time. It will require dedication. It will require willpower. You will need to make healthy decisions. It requires sacrifice. You will need to push your body to its max. There will be temptation. But, I promise you, when you reach your goal, it's worth it."

~ Author Unknown

Your Daily RESET!

How are you pushing yourself today to be the best "you" that you can be? In what areas do you need to push yourself more? Remember, change and growth aren't easy, but it's always worth it.

Day 77

"The smile on my face doesn't mean my life is perfect. It means I appreciate what I have and what God has blessed me with."

~ Author Unknown

Your Daily RESET!

Make a list now of the blessings in your life. Take time to give God thanks for your blessings and recognize He is the giver of all good things and wants only the best for you. Blessings come in all shapes and sizes. Trust that He knows you and will give you the desires of your heart.

Day 78

"Don't be afraid to give up the good and go for the great."

~ Steve Prefontaine

Your Daily RESET!

Think about a time when you settled for something "good" when you knew "great" was just around the corner. What did you learn from that experience?

Day 79

"Let the refining and improving of your own life keep you so busy that you have little time to criticize others."

~ H. Jackson Brown Jr.

Your Daily RESET!

Where is your focus? Is it on being the best you can be or on finding fault in others? Make a commitment today to look first for the strength and potential in others and find ways to cheer them on instead of tear them down.

Day 80

"Stay focused on your destination even if your path may seem stormy today."

~ Billy Cox

Your Daily RESET!

Do you know where you're going in your life? What is your purpose? How are you living your purpose today?

Day 81

"Life is not the way it's supposed to be, it's the way it is. The way you cope with it is what makes the difference."

~ Virginia Satir

Your Daily RESET!

What approaches do you use to effectively deal with adversity in your life? How do you overcome obstacles when they come your way?

Day 82

"I will never apologize for being me, but I will apologize for the times that I am not."

~ Michael Carini

Your Daily RESET!

What words would others use to describe you? What words would you use to describe the "real you"? Where are there similarities? Where are there differences?

Day 83

"No matter how much you revisit the past, there's nothing new to see."

~ Robert Tew

Your Daily RESET!

How easy is it for you to forgive the pain of the past? What's one thing you could do today to let go of a piece of your past that has been difficult to release?

Day 84

"If you want to feel rich just count all the things you have that money cannot buy."

~ Proverb

Your Daily RESET!

Take time to make a list now of the things you have that money cannot buy. If there are people on your list, take some time today to call some of the folks and tell them how much they mean to you. It will radically transform their day...and yours.

Day 85

"It's never too late to be what you might have been."

~ George Eliot

Your Daily RESET!

Who is the real you? What's holding you back from living the "real you" every moment of every day? What is one thing you can do today to let the "real you" shine?

Day 86

"To me, the smell of fresh-made coffee is one of the greatest inventions."

~ Hugh Jackman

Your Daily RESET!

What is your favorite way to relax? Is intentional and focused time to relax part of your daily, weekly, monthly, yearly plan? If not, start today to make it a priority for yourself.

Day 87

> "I think a hero is any person really intent on making this a better place for all people."
>
> ~ Maya Angelou

Your Daily RESET!

Who are some heroes you have known in your life? What made these folks heroes to you? What can you apply from their example to your life?

Day 88

"The greatest danger for most of us is not that our aim is too high and we miss it but that it is too low and we reach it."

~ Michelangelo

Your Daily RESET!

What are you striving to achieve in your life? Is it stretching you to grow or are you settling for mediocre goals and an average life?

Day 89

"The reason we struggle with insecurity is because we compare our behind-the-scenes with everyone else's highlight reel."

~ Steve Furtick

Your Daily RESET!

How much of a struggle is insecurity for you? To what extent do you compare yourself to others, looking at their accomplishments, to judge your own success? Success is nothing more than living your full potential in your unique area of purpose. It is your path alone and cannot be compared to someone else's.

Day 90

"The only certain means of success is to render more and better service than is expected of you, no matter what your task may be."

~ Og Mandino

Your Daily RESET!

Think about a time last week when you didn't receive great service. What do you remember from the experience? Is it easier to remember the times when you had great service or service that was poor? Our natural tendency is to remember the negative rather than the positive. We need to be intentional about giving the best of ourselves in all we do.

Day 91

"You can't do anything about the length of your life, but you can do something about its width and depth."

~ Evan Esar

Your Daily RESET!

What are you doing today to live every moment of your life of purpose with passion, focus, and intentionality?

Day 92

"Your child will follow your example, not your advice."

~ Author Unknown

Your Daily RESET!

What are you modeling to your children today? What do you need to change in your actions to display the message you would want them to hear, see, and learn? If you don't have children, what would you want to model to them? Be intentional in your actions to support the message you would want to share.

Day 93

"Don't be afraid to sit in the front row of your life."

~ Author Unknown

Your Daily RESET!

Are you an active participant in your life or a passive bystander? Do you often times feel life is just passing you by? What's one thing you can do differently today to take an active and intentional role in your life?

Day 94

"Life is an echo. What you send out, comes back. What you sow, you reap. What you give, you get. What you see in others, exists in you."

~ Zig Ziglar

Your Daily RESET!

What is the "voice" of your life? What messages are you sending to those around you?

Day 95

"We need to push the reset button on our lives. We need to evaluate who we are and the choices we are making so we can deliberately and intentionally decide a change is needed in order to live our true purpose and achieve the greatest measure of success."

~ Dr. Jason Brooks

Your Daily RESET!

What is one aspect of your life where you need to push reset? What's one thing you could start doing different today that would make things better for you in this aspect of your life?

Day 96

"Holding a grudge is letting someone live rent-free in your head."

~ Author Unknown

Your Daily RESET!

Are you holding a grudge against someone today? Is there someone you find difficult to forgive? Take time now to write that person's name and what you need to forgive them for. Consider what you would need to release from yourself in order to forgive them.

Day 97

"Take chances, take a lot of them. Because honestly, no matter where you end up and with whom, it always ends up just the way it should be. Your mistakes make you who you are. You learn and grow with each choice you make. Everything is worth it. Say how you feel, always. Be you, and be ok with it."

~ Author Unknown

Your Daily RESET!

Are feelings of regret plaguing your life? Do you find yourself chained to the mistakes of the past and mourning the loss of opportunities? We need to learn from our past but not be held captive to it. What do you need to let go of from your past today?

Day 98

"Always give without remembering and always receive without forgetting."

~ Brian Tracy

Your Daily RESET!

Think back on times in the past when others have given to you and it has been a blessing in your life. If you're still connected with those folks, send them a message today to again thank them for the difference they made in your life.

Day 99

"The only limits in life are the ones you make."

~ Kristinna Habashy

Your Daily RESET!

What limits have you intentionally or unintentionally created in your life? What's one thing you can do today and begin breaking down those limitations?

Day 100

"Focus on your goals. Don't look in any direction but ahead."

~ Author Unknown

Your Daily RESET!

What's holding you back in your life? What do you need to let go of in order to move forward?

Day 101

"There isn't enough room in your mind for both worry and faith. You must decide which one will live there."

~ Author Unknown

Your Daily RESET!

How much space in your mind does worry occupy? Take time now to affirm the positives in your life instead of giving fuel to the worries.

Day 102

"Life is too short to live the same day twice."

~ Diana Perez

Your Daily RESET!

What are you holding onto from you past? What do you need to let go of to forgive yourself or others? Forgiveness brings freedom. Don't be held back any longer by the pain of the past and miss the blessings of the present.

Day 103

"Instead of trying to find yourself, create yourself."

~ George Bernard Shaw

Your Daily RESET!

Who are you becoming today? Remember, every choice you make today is creating the person you will be tomorrow. What do you need to be doing different to be the person you want to be?

Day 104

> "Believe in yourself and all that you are. Know that there is something inside you that is greater than any obstacle."
>
> ~ Christian D. Larson

Your Daily RESET!

How strong is your belief in yourself? How does this belief either move you forward or hold you back on your journey of living your full potential and success?

Day 105

"The key to success is for you to make a habit throughout your life of doing the things you fear."

~ Brian Tracy

Your Daily RESET!

Think about times when you did something that absolutely terrified you? What did you learn about yourself through these experiences?

Day 106

"I used to spend so much time reacting and responding to everyone else that my life had no direction. Other people's lives, problems, and wants set the course for my life. Once I realized it was okay for me to think about and identify what I wanted, remarkable things began to take place in my life."

~ Melody Beattie

Your Daily RESET!

What are you wanting to experience in your life? What are you doing today to help make that experience a reality?

Day 107

"One small Positive thought in the morning can change your whole day."

~ Author Unknown

Your Daily RESET!

Take a few minutes right now to focus on all the things you are grateful for in your life. How does this little redirection in focus change the way you feel right now? Make gratitude a core part of your thoughts today.

Day 108

"Have the courage to follow your heart and intuition. They somehow already know what you truly want to become. Everything else is secondary."

~ Steve Jobs

Your Daily RESET!

Think back on a time when you knew in your heart you should take a certain path, but your head said something different. Which path did you take? What was the result? How difficult is it for you to "trust your gut"? Sometimes, intuition is the best direction.

Day 109

"Don't let someone dim your light, simply because it's shining in their eyes."

~ Author Unknown

Your Daily RESET!

Think back on a time when someone's jealousy of you held you back from doing something you should have done. What did you learn from that experience? How difficult is it for you to live in the fullness of what God created you to be when others are envious of you?

Day 110

"Be so happy that when others look at you they become happy too."

~ Yogi Bhajan

Your Daily RESET!

Take time to think about the things you are saying and doing when you're truly happy. Make it a point to say and do those things today.

Day 111

"By failing to prepare, you are preparing to fail."

~ Benjamin Franklin

Your Daily RESET!

How important is preparation in your life? Do you take time to plan, prepare, and anticipate potential situations? Or, do you just go through the motions and take life as it comes. We can't be so consumed with worry that we don't move forward. But, it is prudent to prepare to the extent that we can see what lies ahead.

Day 112

"People think being alone makes you lonely, but I don't think that's true. Being surrounded by the wrong people is the loneliest thing in the world."

~ Kim Culberston

Your Daily RESET!

Take a few minutes right now to make a list of the people who are closest to you or who you spend the most time with on a daily basis. This could be family, co-workers, friends, neighbors. With this list in mind, are these the right people to be spending your time with? Are they inspiring you to be the best you can be in all areas of your life? You have the ability to choose who you connect and engage with. Make sure you're intentional with your time and relationships.

Day 113

"Two things define you. Your patience when you have nothing, and your attitude when you have everything."

~ Author Unknown

Your Daily RESET!

How are you being intentional with your attitude today?

Day 114

"Success depends less on strength of body than upon strength of mind and character."

~ Arnold Palmer

Your Daily RESET!

Where does your strength come from? Your faith? Your thoughts? Your experiences? Your heart? Your sense of self? All of the above? Find that well of strength and make a point to leverage the strength available to you in every season and circumstance.

Day 115

"Don't judge each day by the harvest you reap but by the seeds that you plant."

~ Robert Louis Stevenson

Your Daily RESET!

What seeds are you planting today? Just like a farmer, we can never be sure what the harvest will be. Sometimes it's abundant. Other times, drought, floods, and other obstacles come and take the harvest away. Our responsibility is to be faithful in the planting where we've been placed and trust God to bring the harvest at the right time.

Day 116

"Take a chance because you'll never know how absolutely perfect something could turn out to be."

~ Author Unknown

Your Daily RESET!

What do you need to take a chance on today? What opportunity is in front of you that you've held off moving forward with even though you know it's what you need to do?

Day 117

"Many people go fishing all their lives without knowing it is not fish they are after."

~ Henry David Thoreau

Your Daily RESET!

What's your life focus? What are you working to accomplish? How does it align with your life purpose? Is there a difference in these for you or are you living in full alignment between your purpose and actions?

Day 118

"We only get what we believe that we deserve. Raise the bar, raise your standards and you will receive a better outcome."

~ Joel Brown

Your Daily RESET!

What do you believe you deserve in your life? Are you continuing to punish yourself for mistakes of the past by saying "Because I did this, I don't deserve to be...". If you believe that statement, it will be difficult to find contentment, freedom, peace, and joy in your life. Let go of the pain of the past and set your eyes on your purpose and the abundant life God has for you ahead.

Day 119

"The secret to having it all is knowing you already do."

~ Author Unknown

Your Daily RESET!

When you think about your life, are you able to celebrate the blessings you've been given? How much time do you spend wishing, hoping, and striving to add "stuff" that ultimately will not satisfy or fulfill?

Day 120

"Not everything will go as you expect in your life. This is why you need to drop expectation, and go with the flow of life."

~ Leon Brown

Your Daily RESET!

Think back on the last week. Remember a situation that didn't go as you had planned. What were you thinking through that experience? What were you feeling through the experience? How did you handle it? What did you learn from it?

Day 121

"Surround yourself with the dreamers and the doers, the believers and thinkers, but most of all, surround yourself with those who see greatness within you, even when you don't see it yourself."

~ Edmund Lee

Your Daily RESET!

Who are you surrounding yourself with? Do they inspire you to live your full potential and be everything you were created to be?

Day 122

"The greatest fulfillment comes when our individual paths connect in such a way that we can share in the experiences of others while pursuing our own purpose and ultimate success."

~ Dr. Jason Brooks

Your Daily RESET!

In what ways are you pouring yourself into someone else's life today to help them be all they can be? The reality is we never learn as much as when we teach, coach, and mentor others.

Day 123

"What is your 'To Be' List?"

~ Lauren Rosenfeld and James McMahon

Your Daily RESET!

What do you want "To Be"? Make the list now. What areas of your life need to change in order to make your "To Be" list a reality?

Day 124

"The worst enemy to creativity is self-doubt."

~ Sylvia Plath

Your Daily RESET!

Do you believe in yourself? Do you have faith you can persevere and build the life you've imagined? Do you trust everything happens for a reason and God works even challenging times for our good?

Day 125

"Realize deeply that the present moment is all you ever have."

~ Eckhart Tolle

Your Daily RESET!

How difficult is it for you to be totally present in the moment? Take time now to close your eyes, breathe deeply, and give thanks for "the present" of this moment.

Day 126

"The most important decision you will ever make is what you do with the time that is given to you."

~ Author Unknown

Your Daily RESET!

Are you intentional with the time that's been given to you? We've all been given 86,400 seconds each day by God to live, learn, love, and leave a legacy. What are you doing with the time that's been given to you?

Day 127

"Balance, peace, and joy are the fruit of a successful life. It starts with recognizing your talents and finding ways to serve others by using them."

~ Thomas Kinkade

Your Daily RESET!

What are your talents? What have you been given to serve others? Who can you serve today through your talents?

Day 128

"Never quit. If you stumble, get back up. What happened yesterday no longer matters. Today's another day. So, get back on track and move closer to your dreams and goals. You can do it."

~ Patrick Higgins

Your Daily RESET!

What's the next step you need to take today to move closer to living your purpose with passion?

Day 129

"Don't listen to people who tell you what to do. Listen to people who encourage you to do what you know in your heart is right."

~ Author Unknown

Your Daily RESET!

Who are the encouragers in your life? Reach out today and thank them for their encouragement and support.

Day 130

> "The happiest people don't have the best of everything, they just make the best of everything."
>
> ~ Sam Cawthorn

Your Daily RESET!

Think about your life. Are you happy where you are? Instead of seeking happiness, can you find joy, contentment, and peace where you are right now? There is a difference. Happiness is an emotion...joy, contentment and peace are attitudes. You can choose you attitude...choose wisely.

Day 131

"We are what we repeatedly do."

~ Aristotle

Your Daily RESET!

Where are your habits taking you? Are they moving you closer to your dreams or further away? What habits do you need to change in your life to be more successful?

Day 132

"Stop saying 'I wish'. Start saying 'I will'."

~ David Copperfield

Your Daily RESET!

"Wish" is just a dream. "Will" is a definite course and action leading to results. What "will" you do different today? Now, do it!

Day 133

"I can be changed by what happens to me. But I refuse to be reduced by it."

~ Maya Angelou

Your Daily RESET!

Who have you become as a result of your past? What changes need to come in your attitudes, thoughts, and actions to become who you want to be?

Day 134

"Don't let your past steal your future. Move on."

~ Author Unknown

Your Daily RESET!

How difficult is it for you to move forward from the pain of the past? We must find the strength to forgive and move on.

Day 135

> "Be willing to risk failure in pursuit of what you believe in. Not every success occurred overnight. Rather SUCCESS is typically born of great sacrifice and overcoming adversity."
>
> ~ Author Unknown

Your Daily RESET!

Think back on a time when you were successful in your life. Did the success you achieved come easy or did it require an investment from you to accomplish? Remember, we often appreciate more the things that cost us something to obtain rather than those which come easy.

Day 136

"If you do what you've always done you'll get what you've always gotten."

~ Anthony Robbins

Your Daily RESET!

Take time now to make a list of the things you've done in the past, or are doing now, you know are holding you back from being all you were created to be. Choose one from the list and commit to doing something different today.

Day 137

"Our background and circumstances may have influenced who we are, but we are responsible for who we become."

~ James Rhineheart

Your Daily RESET!

How is your past holding you back from the future you want to create for yourself? Do you have folks you need to forgive in order to move forward with your life? Remember, we are a product of our past but we don't need to be a prisoner to it. You can choose!

Day 138

"The only person you are destined to become is the person you decide to be."

~ Ralph Waldo Emerson

Your Daily RESET!

Take a few minutes right now to write down the characteristics of the person you want to be. Now, on a scale of 1 to 10, evaluate to what degree you are truly living each of these desired characteristics. What could you do different in just one of these areas to be better for yourself today?

Day 139

"Good things are coming down the road. Just don't stop walking."

~ Robert Warren Painter, Jr.

Your Daily RESET!

Think back on times when you went through painful seasons. What was it that got you through those difficult times? Those are all experiences to help you build strength. What steps do you need to take today to start moving forward in an area of your life where you are stuck?

Day 140

"Nothing is more expensive than a missed opportunity."

~ H. Jackson Brown, Jr.

Your Daily RESET!

What opportunities are you seeing today that you need to take? What's standing in your way of moving forward? Make the decision and commitment today to take the next step.

Day 141

"Never get so busy making a living that you forget to make a life."

~ Dolly Parton

Your Daily RESET!

What's the life you're making for yourself? If others were looking at how you spend your time, talent, treasure, and talk, what would they say is most important to you?

Day 142

"Always believe that something wonderful is about to happen."

~ Author Unknown

Your Daily RESET!

Do you believe God has the best in mind for you and wants you to experience a wonderful life? Give thanks for the opportunities you have today and for those in the future which you cannot yet see.

Day 143

"Each moment of every day, you have a choice to make. You can choose to live in fear, defeat, and doubt. Or, you can choose to live in faith and confidence that this moment was created for you to help you be all you were created to be."

~ Dr. Jason Brooks

Your Daily RESET!

Make a list of 5 things you want said about the life you live. What's one thing you need to be doing different today to bring this quick vision of your life into reality and focus?

Day 144

"Comparison is the thief of joy."

~ Theodore Roosevelt

Your Daily RESET!

How often do you compare yourself to others? What benefit do you gain from comparing yourself to others? If there are no or few benefits, why do you do it? Commit today to spend less time comparing yourself to others and more being authentic to yourself.

Day 145

"Face trouble with courage, disappointment with cheerfulness, and triumph with humility."

~ Thomas S. Monson

Your Daily RESET!

In what ways are you living with courage, cheerfulness, and humility?

Day 146

"Dear past, thank you for your lessons. Dear future, I'm ready. Dear God, thank you for giving me another chance."

~ Author Unknown

Your Daily RESET!

Give thanks for at least one thing from your past and give thanks to God for the opportunities ahead to live, lead, learn, love, and leave a legacy.

Day 147

"The only way to do great work is to love what you do."

~ Steve Jobs

Your Daily RESET!

Do you feel fulfilled in your work? Do you know you're making a difference and contributing meaningfully for a greater good? What's the contribution you are making today through your work? The vast majority of people go through each day plodding along, not really energized or motivated by their work, because it doesn't align with their purpose and they really don't know how they're making a difference. You can walk a different path. Commit today to starting the journey to learning and living your purpose with passion!

Day 148

"Everybody is a genius. But if you judge a fish by its ability to climb a tree, it will live its whole life believing that it is stupid."

~ Albert Einstein

Your Daily RESET!

How are you evaluating your success? Do you compare your accomplishments to the accomplishments of others? Or, do you compare your progress against your potential? Playing the comparison game with others will only lead to frustration, jealousy, resentment, and envy. You were uniquely created to live your life. Living your potential to the fullest is the true measure of success.

Day 149

> "Success is the sum of small efforts, repeated day in and day out."
>
> ~ R. Collier

Your Daily RESET!

What are the success habits you've built into your life? What habits do you have that are not leading you to success? What habits do you need to change? Be intentional with your life in the small actions of the day.

Day 150

> "In the end, the greatest measure of success – your success – is how you are living each and every minute in alignment with your purpose."
>
> ~ Dr. Jason Brooks

Your Daily RESET!

Do you know what your purpose is…or the reason you are alive today? If so, write it down now. If not, what's one thing you could do today to start on the journey to identifying your purpose? Make the decision now to take that step.

Day 151

"Remember happiness is a way of travel, not a destination."

~ Roy Goodman

Your Daily RESET!

How prevalent is happiness in your life? The moments we experience may not all be happy but we can choose our response to our situations and bring us back to happiness more quickly. Think about a difficult aspect of your life right now. Say to yourself, "Although this situation is difficult, I choose joy and believe that God is working all things together for my good." Just this little change could make all the difference.

Day 152

"Life is way too short to spend another day at war with yourself."

~ Author Unknown

Your Daily RESET!

In what ways are you battling with yourself? What do you need to surrender to be able to move forward with your life and pursue the dreams God has for you?

Day 153

"It always seems impossible until it's done."

~ Nelson Mandela

Your Daily RESET!

Think back on something you thought was not possible for you to do that you eventually accomplished. What did you learn from the experience? How did you grow? What did you take from the experience you can apply to situations today you see as impossible?

Day 154

> "Don't be afraid to fail. Be afraid not to try."
>
> ~ Michael Jordan

Your Daily RESET!

Think back on a time when you tried something that scared you. What was it? What did you learn about yourself through the experience you can apply to scary situations you're facing today? Most often although something may be scary to us, it's never as bad as what we fear it will be. Keep moving on!

Day 155

"Everything you want in life is just one step away; all you have to do is decide in which direction to step."

~ Author Unknown

Your Daily RESET!

What is a step you need to take today that you have been reluctant to take? Don't let the Law of Diminishing Intent hold you back any longer. Take the next step.

Day 156

"To change bad habits, we must study the habits of successful role models."

~ Jack Canfield

Your Daily RESET!

Who are your role models? What are the five to six habits that make them successful? Which of those habits would make sense for you to start doing? What can you begin today to bring some of those healthy habits into your life? What do you need to stop doing that's holding you back?

Day 157

"The positive thinker sees the invisible, feels the intangible and achieves the impossible."

~ Winston Churchill

Your Daily RESET!

Remember a time when you chose positive instead of negative thoughts in a challenging situation. What did you learn from the experience? How can making positive thoughts the dominant influence in your life make a difference for you today?

Day 158

"Success in life is never achieved without confidence for today and courage for the future."

~ Dr. Jason Brooks

Your Daily RESET!

What does confidence mean to you? What does courage mean to you? How big a part does confidence and courage play in your life? Are you willing to take the next right step into the unknown and face the challenges of uncertainty?

Day 159

"Nothing is beneath you if it is in the direction of your life."

~ Ralph Waldo Emerson

Your Daily RESET!

How clear are you on the direction you desire for your life? Are you living each moment in alignment with that vision? What do you need to start doing…or stop doing today so you can be more in line with your life vision?

Day 160

"Your life is your message to the world. Make sure it's inspiring."

~ Lorrin L. Lee

Your Daily RESET!

What's the message your life is sending to the world? Is it inspiring, encouraging, and motivating or sad, defeated, and demoralized? You are writing a story with every moment of your life. Make it a great one.

Day 161

"Balance is not something you find, it's something you create."

~ Jana Kingsford

Your Daily RESET!

What does life balance mean to you? What does life balance look like for you? Do you want a greater degree of balance and wellness? In what ways are you creating balance in your life today? How challenging is it for you to create and maintain healthy balance and wellness?

Day 162

"Sometimes a single word can make all the difference."

~ Joyce Meyer

Your Daily RESET!

Focus on the word "Joy" today. What does it mean to you? How are you bringing joy into your life? Intentionally look for ways to share joy with others today.

Day 163

"As I look back on my life, I realize that every time I thought I was being rejected from something good, I was actually being re-directed to something better."

~ Steve Maraboli

Your Daily RESET!

Think back on and make a list of some times in your life when, although at the time you thought you were being rejected, ultimately everything turned out better than you could have possibly imagined. Take time now to give thanks for those times of redirection.

Day 164

"Make mistakes, take chances, be silly, be imperfect, trust yourself and follow your heart."

~ Author Unknown

Your Daily RESET!

When was the last time you took a risk and jumped into the deep water? What's one thing you could do today to stretch yourself and risk making a growth-giving mistake?

Day 165

"Gratitude unlocks the fullness of life. It turns what we have into enough and more. It turns denial into acceptance, chaos to order, confusion to clarity. It can turn a meal into a feast, a house into a home, a stranger into a friend. Gratitude makes sense of our past, brings peace for today, and creates a vision for tomorrow."

~ Melody Beattie

Your Daily RESET!

What are you grateful for from your past? What are you grateful for today?

Day 166

"Nothing binds you except your thoughts; nothing limits you except your fear; and nothing controls you except your beliefs."

~ Marianne Williamson

Your Daily RESET!

Think back on a time when your thoughts limited your ability to move forward with confidence. What did you learn from the experience? How can you apply that learning today to a situation you're facing that brings you fear?

Day 167

"Everyone desires success but few know how to chart the path to achieve it. Those who really understand the idea of success and pursue their unique vision of success daily have a special energy and enthusiasm that's immediately evident and inspiring to everyone they meet."

~ Dr. Jason Brooks

Your Daily RESET!

What does success look like for you? Make a list of the things you would be thinking, doing, feeling, and believing that would let you know you are successful.

Day 168

"The only person you should try to be better than is the person you were yesterday."

~ Author Unknown

Your Daily RESET!

What are you doing to invest in your self-development?

Day 169

"This life is a gift but it only comes one day at a time. Each morning we open the 'present' anew and make the choice of what we are going to do with it today."

~ Dr. Jason Brooks

Your Daily RESET!

What are you going to do with the "present" of today? Are you going to open it, embrace it, and enjoy it to the fullest? Or, are you going to leave it wrapped and sealed, never knowing the incredible joy it can bring? The choice is yours.

Day 170

"Every morning you have two choices: continue to sleep with your dreams, or wake up and chase them."

~ Author Unknown

Your Daily RESET!

What dreams are you waiting to chase in your life? What's holding you back? What is one thing you can begin doing today to start moving in the direction of pursuing your dreams?

Day 171

"It's surprising how many persons go through life without ever recognizing that their feelings toward other people are largely determined by their feelings toward themselves, and if you're not comfortable within yourself, you can't be comfortable with others."

~ Sidney J. Harris

Your Daily RESET!

How comfortable are you with yourself? Make a list of the 5 things you like most about yourself. Take time today to celebrate those strengths.

Day 172

"Surround yourself with positive successful people."

~ Author Unknown

Your Daily RESET!

What characteristics do you want to see in people you surround yourself with? Think about the 5 closest people to you? Do they have those characteristics? Are you compromising on your "friend standards"? What changes do you need to make today?

Day 173

"Own your words. Own your actions. Be aware of what you are putting out there."

~ Sheila Burke

Your Daily RESET!

Do you take responsibility for your life? Or, do you pass responsibility to others and make excuses? Ultimately, only you are responsible for what you say and what you do. Be intentional, aware, and remember there are consequences, good or bad, to everything we say and do.

Day 174

"Life doesn't always go according to plan. Sometimes heading in a new direction can be scary until you realize you're headed toward a new and exciting destination."

~ Susan Gale

Your Daily RESET!

Think back on a time when things didn't go according to plan. What was that like for you? In what ways did you grow through that experience?

Day 175

"Do it now. Sometimes 'later' becomes 'never'."

~ Author Unknown

Your Daily RESET!

What have you been meaning to do that you have not yet started? What's one thing you can do today to start moving forward?

Day 176

"If you don't like where you are, then change it. You are not a tree."

~ Jim Rohn

Your Daily RESET!

Do you feel stuck in an area of your life that just hasn't quite turned out the way you had hoped? The reality is you're not stuck...you can choose to move. Move away from a painful relationship or a challenging situation. Make the choice today to do one thing different.

Day 177

"When faced with two choices, simply toss a coin. It works not because it settles the question for you, but because in that brief moment when the coin is in the air, you suddenly know what you are hoping for."

~ Author Unknown

Your Daily RESET!

How difficult is it for you to make decisions in your life? Do you often feel so conflicted and confused that it's tough for you to commit to a direction? Do you often find yourself second-guessing your decisions, wondering if a different choice would have been better?

Day 178

"The day you decide that you are more interested in being aware of your thoughts than you are in the thoughts themselves – that is the day you will find your way out."

~ Michael Singer

Your Daily RESET!

Do you find yourself often surprised by the thoughts that are taking up residence in your mind? Do you often wonder where the thoughts come from? Self-awareness of thoughts and how those thoughts impact your life is the beginning of taking full responsibility for yourself and developing total intelligence.

Day 179

"Today's circumstances do not define you. God's plans for your life are so much greater."

~ Gwen Smith

Your Daily RESET!

Do you believe God has a great purpose and plan for you? If not, what's standing in your way of believing in this truth?

Day 180

"You don't get what you wish for. You get what you work for."

~ Author Unknown

Your Daily RESET!

How do you balance dreaming and action in your life? All the great ideas and dreams without action are lost.

Day 181

"Our daily focus should be on achieving progress, not perfection."

~ Dr. Jason Brooks

Your Daily RESET!

In what ways are you investing in yourself today? Are you intentionally taking steps to learn and grow? Progress should be our goal every day…progress toward becoming the full-person God created us to be and living His purpose for our lives.

Day 182

"Straight roads do not make skillful drivers."

~ Paulo Coelho

Your Daily RESET!

What twists and turns in your life have helped you to become who you are today? What did you learn from those experiences that you can apply to situations you're facing now?

Day 183

"The greatest pleasure in life is doing what people say you cannot do."

~ Walter Bagehot

Your Daily RESET!

When have you overcome others opinions of you and achieved beyond what you ever imagined? What should you do today to stretch beyond yourself?

Day 184

"Be confident. Too many days are wasted comparing ourselves to others and wishing to be something we aren't. Everybody has their own strengths and weaknesses, and it is only when you accept everything you are - and aren't - that you will truly succeed."

~ Author Unknown

Your Daily RESET!

On a scale of 1 to 10, how would you evaluate your degree of confidence? Is it challenging for you to be confident in familiar situations. How about in new situations? What's one thing you could do different to build confidence in yourself?

Day 185

"The biggest communication problem is we do not listen to understand. We listen to reply."

~ Author Unknown

Your Daily RESET!

How much of a struggle is this for you? Intentionally focus today on "listening to understand"...deeply understand...instead of listening to reply.

Day 186

"Never give up on a dream just because of the time it will take to accomplish it. The time will pass anyway."

~ Earl Nightingale

Your Daily RESET!

What dreams do you have in your life that you have almost given up on? If you truly believe with all your heart this is a dream that has been placed inside you by God, He will bring it to pass. Don't give up. Trust in Him. Take the next step.

> Day 187

> "A head full of fears has no space for dreams."
>
> ~ Author Unknown

Your Daily RESET!

How are fears in your life crushing your dreams? What fears do you need to actively reject and remove from your life? How could the release from fear free you to live your dreams?

Day 188

"Be brave. You've got this!"

~ Author Unknown

Your Daily RESET!

Think back on a time when you faced your fears and moved forward into a challenging situation with confidence and courage. What did you learn about yourself? You're stronger than you think. Take the challenges that come your way today and trust you have all you need to succeed.

Day 189

"Balance is not better time management, but better boundary management. Balance means making choices and enjoying those choices."

~ Betsy Jacobson

Your Daily RESET!

What boundaries have you established in your life? Do you have clear non-negotiables that are important for you and your family? Are the boundaries you've set leading toward you living a balanced and healthy life? If not, make the needed changes today.

Day 190

"Live in the present, launch yourself on every wave, find eternity in each moment..."

~ Henry David Thoreau

Your Daily RESET!

Where do you invest the majority of your thoughts…on reviewing the past, dreaming of the future, or living in the present? In reality, we only have this moment in our lives. How are you living each moment to the fullest?

Day 191

"Everything in life...has to have balance."

~ Donna Karan

Your Daily RESET!

Do you feel out of balance in your life? Do you feel out of control? You can create greater balance and wellness in your life, but it takes focus, determination, and discipline. What are you willing to do to achieve greater balance in your life?

Day 192

"If you want to make your dreams come true, the first thing you have to do is wake up."

~ J.M. Power

Your Daily RESET!

Some people spend so much time dreaming that they don't take action. What's one thing you need to do today to move forward to accomplish something you've had on the back burner of your life for some time?

Day 193

"Accept your past without regret, handle your present with confidence, and face your future without fear."

~ Author Unknown

Your Daily RESET!

Do you have regrets from your past? How are those holding you back from living fully in the present with confidence and embracing your future without fear? God is waiting to free you from your regrets and lead you into the full life He created for you.

Day 194

"Ask yourself this question: 'Will this matter a year from now?'"

~ Richard Carlson

Your Daily RESET!

How intentional are you about the things you're doing today? The decisions you make today with what you do with your time, talent, talk, and treasure will create who you will be in the future and the legacy you leave.

Day 195

"You can't live a positive life with a negative mind."

~ Author Unknown

Your Daily RESET!

How prevalent are negative thoughts in your life? How often do you find yourself slipping into a negative mindset? Make a commitment today that when negative thoughts start to come into your mind to acknowledge them, capture them, and replace them with positive thoughts of praise, gratitude, and possibilities.

Day 196

"Every day you must unlearn the ways that hold you back. You must rid yourself of negativity, so you can learn to fly."

~ Leon Brown

Your Daily RESET!

What are some areas of your life where you experience feelings of negativity? What positive thoughts and feelings can you use to replace the negative?

Day 197

"The more you express gratitude for what you have, the more things you'll have to express gratitude for."

~ Zig Ziglar

Your Daily RESET!

Make a list of the 10 things in your life you are most grateful for. If there are people on your list, let them know you're thankful for them today.

Day 198

"Some succeed because they are destined to, but most succeed because they are determined to."

~ Henry Van Dyke

Your Daily RESET!

What are you willing to do to achieve success in your life? What are you willing to invest of yourself? What are you willing to sacrifice?

Day 199

"Average people have wishes and hopes. Confident, courageous, and successful people have goals and plans."

~ Dr. Jason Brooks

Your Daily RESET!

Think back on a time when you modeled confidence and courage in your life. What were the results when you applied confidence and courage to a challenging situation? In what areas of your life do you need to demonstrate more confidence and courage today?

Day 200

"Opportunity is missed by people because it is dressed in overalls and looks like work."

~ Thomas Edison

Your Daily RESET!

What opportunities are you missing today because you're not willing to do what it takes to make it happen? Often we want to take the easy road and miss opportunities that are hidden in commitment and hard work. Success often requires sacrifice. What do you need to give of yourself today to make your dreams a reality?

Day 201

"Life is like riding a bicycle. To keep your balance, you must keep moving."

~ Albert Einstein

Your Daily RESET!

How are you moving forward today with creating balance and wellness in your life? Are you making intentional decisions to build balance and wellness or just going through the motions believing tomorrow will be better without intentional action today?

Day 202

"Do something today that your future self will thank you for."

~ Author Unknown

Your Daily RESET!

What's one thing you could do today that will be an investment in you? Do it!

Day 203

"If not you, who?"

~ Author Unknown

Your Daily RESET!

How long will you wait for someone else to do something that you know in your heart you should be doing to touch the lives of others?

Day 204

"During times of challenge and change, we have choices to make. We can allow our feelings of loss and unmet expectations to consume us or we can reset by viewing our life through the new lens of opportunity and hope for an amazing future. The choice is yours!"

~ Dr. Jason Brooks

Your Daily RESET!

Is it difficult for you to see opportunity and potential in every situation? Do you often find yourself consumed by feelings of loss when things don't work out the way you had hoped, or trying to hold on so tight to what you have that it's almost suffocating? How difficult would it be for you to reset?

Day 205

"On any given day you can massively change the direction of your life."

~ Author Unknown

Your Daily RESET!

Is there a new direction you would like to take in an area of your life that's not working out the way you had hoped? What's one thing you could do different today that would be better for you in that area?

Day 206

"You cannot change your destination overnight, but you can change your direction overnight."

~ Jim Rohn

Your Daily RESET!

Where are you going in your life? Do you have a clear picture of your desired destination? What's one thing you could be doing differently today to take a next step toward reaching your desired destination? Now…do it!

Day 207

"The more you know who you are, and what you want, the less you let things upset you."

~ Bob Harris

Your Daily RESET!

How often do you feel upset or disappointed by the way things happen in your life? Do you often feel rejected and off course? This could be a result of not having clarity for yourself, your purpose, or the course you should be taking.

Day 208

"If it scares you, it might be a good thing to try."

~ Seth Godin

Your Daily RESET!

Think back on a time when you did something that scared you and stretched you. What did you learn from the experience? What have you been avoiding doing because it scares you?

Day 209

"The hardest thing in life is knowing which bridge to cross and which to burn."

~ David Russell

Your Daily RESET!

What relationships have you kept that you know are not healthy for you? What steps should you take today to either move from the relationship or make the relationship better?

Day 210

"Never give up on what you really want to do. The person with big dreams is more powerful than one with all the facts."

~ Albert Einstein

Your Daily RESET!

Make a list of the 5 things you are dreaming to accomplish in your life. What's one step you could take today that would move you closer to seeing your dreams come to reality? Do it!

Day 211

> "But now, O Lord, you are our Father;
> We are the clay, and you our Potter;
> And we are all the work of your hand."

Isaiah 64:8, *The Holy Bible (ESV)*

Your Daily RESET!

Did you know you were specifically made for a purpose and created for a great work? God knew you before you were born. What is your purpose? How are you living your purpose each and every day?

"If not now, when?"

~ Author Unknown

Your Daily RESET!

How long will you continue to wait to move forward with something you know you need to do?

Day 213

"Today is the first blank page of a 365 page book. Write a good one!"

~ Author Unknown

Your Daily RESET!

What's the story of your life? Is it an intimate love story? An epic adventure? A situational comedy? Whatever your story…make it a good one.

Day 214

"When you want to succeed as bad as you want to breathe, then you will be successful."

~ Eric Thomas

Your Daily RESET!

Where does your passion for success come from? Are you driven to live your full potential each moment and unwilling to accept anything less? Success is different for everyone but each of us must commit all we are and all we do to pursuing that success with intentionality every day.

Day 215

*"Act as if what you do makes a difference.
It does."*

~ William James

Your Daily RESET!

How intentional are you with your choices and actions? Are you consciously choosing the steps to take through the day or letting circumstances, situations, and other people chart your course? Make a commitment now to be intentional with every moment today.

Day 216

"It's kind of fun to do the impossible."

~ Walt Disney

Your Daily RESET!

Think back on a time when you accomplished something you believed was impossible. What was it like for you? How can you apply that feeling and motivation to an impossible situation you're facing today?

Day 217

"Everyone you meet is fighting a battle you know nothing about. Be kind. Always."

~ Wendy Mass

Your Daily RESET!

What can you do today to reach out to someone in need?

Day 218

"You can do anything, but not everything."

~ David Allen

Your Daily RESET!

Do you find yourself overwhelmed by trying to do too much? Often, people actually accomplish very little because they stretch themselves too thin...trying to do everything. If you keep your life simple and stay focused, you will be amazed at what you accomplish, one small step at a time.

Day 219

"What consumes your mind, controls your life."

~ Creed

Your Daily RESET!

Take time right now to make a list of your dominant thoughts. In what ways are those thoughts lifting you up? In what ways are they bringing you down? What thoughts need to change for your life to be better?

Day 220

"When you want something you've never had, you have to do something you've never done."

~ Thomas Jefferson

Your Daily RESET!

What's something in your life you're striving to obtain that you've never had? What are you going to have to do to make this a reality?

Day 221

"Always end the day with a positive thought. No matter how hard things were, tomorrow's a fresh opportunity to make it better."

~ Author Unknown

Your Daily RESET!

If this isn't already part of your daily habits, start a praise journal tonight. Before you go to sleep, make a list of three things you're thankful for in your life. You will be amazed at how this helps you to rest, clear your mind, and start fresh in the morning.

Day 222

"The most influential persuasion tool you have in your entire arsenal is your integrity."

~ Zig Ziglar

Your Daily RESET!

What does integrity mean to you? Is integrity important to you? How do you live a life of integrity with yourself and others?

Day 223

"I am strong because I know my weaknesses. I am beautiful because I am aware of my flaws. I am fearless because I learned to recognize illusion from reality. I am wise because I learn from my mistakes. I am a lover because I have felt hate. I can laugh because I have known sadness."

~ Author Unknown

Your Daily RESET!

The reality is we all have weaknesses or areas we would like to improve in our lives. What are some of your weaknesses? In what ways have you gained strength in the past despite your weaknesses to overcome challenges you've faced?

Day 224

"Add life to your days, not days to your life."

~ Sangamithra Gangarapu

Your Daily RESET!

How are you making the most of each day you live? How are you making the most of today? Are you living with intentionality or just floating through life? Be radical...be intentional!

Day 225

"A good life is when you assume nothing, do more, need less, smile often, dream big, laugh a lot, and realize how blessed you are."

~ Author Unknown

Your Daily RESET!

How do you define a life of success? What does a life of success look like to you? What would you be thinking, feeling, saying, and doing to let you know you were successful? What could you start doing differently today to move toward your picture of success?

Day 226

"Tell everyone what you want to do and someone will want to help you do it."

~ W. Clement Stone

Your Daily RESET!

How easy is it for you to be open and honest with others about your dreams? Do you have trusted friends you can share your goals with? Over the next seven days, take time to share with five people what you plan to accomplish over the next year and see what opportunities come from those conversations to help you move forward.

Day 227

"The sky is not the limit. Your imagination is."

~ Author Unknown

Your Daily RESET!

What are you imagining today? What are you dreaming for yourself? For your family? For your friends?

Day 228

"Doubt kills more dreams than failure ever will."

~ Author Unknown

Your Daily RESET!

In what ways does doubt have a hold on you today? What's one thing you can do differently to help break the chains of doubt and uncertainty in your life?

Day 229

"Forget all the reasons why it won't work and believe the one reason why it will."

~ Author Unknown

Your Daily RESET!

What are you dreaming for in your life? Select one of your dreams and make a list of the obstacles that could stand in the way of you bringing this dream into reality. Now, make a list of the things you could do or the people you need to help you overcome those obstacles. If God puts a dream and vision in your heart, at just the right time, He will provide all you need to make the dream come alive.

Day 230

"I forgive myself for not being perfect. I recognize we're all not perfect. I am open to forgiving others. I value persistence, insights, and growth far more than perfection."

~ Author Unknown

Your Daily RESET!

How difficult is it for you to forgive yourself? Often, self-forgiveness is more challenging than forgiving others because we know all the deep, dark secrets of our failures. You were never meant to live with shame, guilt, and feelings of failure. God is with you, ready to forgive you, right where you are. When you fully experience and embrace His unconditional forgiveness, you can truly forgive yourself.

Day 231

"Life without direction, life without purpose, life without intent, will surely rob you of your legacy. Go make waves!"

~ Chris Holmes

Your Daily RESET!

What's the legacy you want to leave? What do you want the story of your life to be? Make a list of the ten things you would want said about you when your life is over. Are you living today in a way that would be in alignment with your vision for your life and the story you want to be told?

Day 232

"Before you act, listen. Before you react, think. Before you spend, earn. Before you criticize, wait. Before you pray, forgive. Before you quit, try."

~ Ernest Hemingway

Your Daily RESET!

How are you being intentional with every moment, thought, action, and relationship today?

Day 233

"No matter how busy you may think you are, you must find time for reading, or surrender yourself to self-chosen ignorance."

~ Confucius

Your Daily RESET!

What's the last book you read? You are either green and growing or ripe and rotting. Take the first step to invest in yourself today.

Day 234

"Failure is only the opportunity to begin again, only this time more wisely."

~ Henry Ford

Your Daily RESET!

Think back on a time when you were not successful at something you tried. What did you learn from the experience? How are you applying that learning to your life today? Nothing happens by accident and all experiences can be used to build and inspire us if we only recognize and embrace the value of the experience – good or bad.

Day 235

"You are the storyteller of your life. It is up to you, and you alone to determine the path in which your life takes. You can either live a life of mediocrity or you can live a life worth remembering. You are in direct control of the type of legacy that you will leave. Remember that!"

~ Edmund S. Lee

Your Daily RESET!

What has been the story of your life? What do you want the story to be? What's one thing you can do different today to begin a new chapter and create a new ending?

Day 236

"The best way to predict the future is to create it."

~ Peter Drucker

Your Daily RESET!

What future are you creating based on your actions today? What actions need to change to create the future you desire? For example, if you're filling your diet with fast food, your future will hold challenges with your physical health. Is that what you want? If not, change today.

Day 237

> "Every time we choose safety, we reinforce fear."
>
> ~ Cheri Huber

Your Daily RESET!

In what ways is fear holding you back from accomplishments in your life? What can you do today to resist and overcome the fear in your life and press on to achieve greatness? Often it takes only a single step. What will that step be for you today?

Day 238

"The most dangerous risk of all – the risk of spending your life not doing what you want on the bet you can buy yourself the freedom to do it later."

~ Randy Komisar

Your Daily RESET!

How much time do you spend doing what you don't want to do in hopes that at some point in the future, you will have the freedom to do everything you want to do? Every moment is an investment in the future. What future are you creating for yourself?

Day 239

"When everything seems to be going against you, remember that the airplane takes off against the wind, not with it."

~ Henry Ford

Your Daily RESET!

Think back on a time when struggles you faced actually resulted in an opportunily to grow. What did you learn from the experience? How are you better today as a result?

Day 240

"It's okay to have flaws. They make you real."

~ Ziad K. Abdelnour

Your Daily RESET!

How easy is it for you to acknowledge your flaws, accept your flaws, and love yourself in spite of your flaws knowing you were purposefully created just the way you are? Are you willing to be transparent enough to allow your flaws to be used to inspire others to persevere and grow through their struggles?

Day 241

"More people would learn from their mistakes if they weren't so busy denying them."

~ Harold J. Smith

Your Daily RESET!

Make a list of some of the "mistakes" you've made in the last three months. What did you learn from those mistakes? How have you applied those learnings to your life?

Day 242

"You can never cross the ocean unless you have the courage to lose sight of the shore."

~ Christopher Columbus

Your Daily RESET!

Think about a time when you had the courage to let go of the safety of the shore and risk the opportunities of a new adventure. What did you learn from the experience?

Day 243

"Never look down on someone unless you're helping them up."

~ Jesse Jackson

Your Daily RESET!

Think about the people you encounter on a daily basis. Do you most often view them through a lens of judgment or acceptance? What can you do to lift someone up today?

Day 244

"You cannot control what happens to you, but you can control your attitude toward what happens to you, and in that, you will be mastering change rather than allowing it to master you."

~ Brian Tracy

Your Daily RESET!

What attitude changes do you need to make in order to create the best life possible?

Day 245

"Your hardest times often lead to the greatest moments of your life. Keep the faith. It will all be worth it in the end."

~ Author Unknown

Your Daily RESET!

Think back on a challenging time in your life. What did you learn from the experience? In what ways did you grow as a result of the situation?

Day 246

"A pessimist sees the difficulty in every opportunity. An optimist sees the opportunity in every difficulty."

~ Winston Churchill

Your Daily RESET!

Which are you most like, the pessimist or the optimist? How challenging is it for you to see the positives and opportunities in situations, particularly difficult situations?

Day 247

"You will not get what you truly deserve if you're too attached to the things you're supposed to let go of."

~ Author Unknown

Your Daily RESET!

What do you need to let go of in your life? What are you holding tightly to today that keeps you from opening your hands to receive something better that's waiting for you? Often, we will hold onto the things that are familiar, even though they are painful for us, because we struggle with change. Take the first step today to let go. God has an incredible life in store for you if you just let go and trust Him to lead.

Day 248

> "People's lives are a direct reflection of the expectations of their peer group."
>
> ~ Anthony Robbins

Your Daily RESET!

Think about the six people who are closest to you. Write down their names. Now, write down some of their traits and characteristics. How do those align with who you are and who you want to be?

Day 249

"Invest in yourself first. Expect nothing from no one and be willing to work for everything."

~ Tony Gaskins

Your Daily RESET!

In what ways are you investing in yourself? Remember, you are either green and growing or ripe and rotting. There is no status quo.

Day 250

"We have been given two gifts..time and choice. We have the ability to choose what we will do with our time and every minute we use will be accounted for."

~ Dr. Jason Brooks

Your Daily RESET!

We are unique from any other part of God's creation. Everything else is subject to seasons of time and instincts that are created in them for those seasons. For example, when winter comes, bears hibernate. It's in their DNA. Humans, however, have a choice as to what we will do each and every day. How are you taking responsibility for the choices you're making today?

Day 251

> "The best and safest thing is to keep a balance in your life, acknowledge the great powers around us and in us. If you can do that, and live that way, you are really wise."
>
> ~ Euripides

Your Daily RESET!

Life balance is possible, but it requires focus and discipline. God created us for balance and He gives us the ability to evaluate and make course corrections that are needed. What areas of your life feel out of balance today? What's one thing you could do different to make your life better?

Day 252

"We can complain because rose bushes have thorns, or rejoice because thorn bushes have roses."

~ Abraham Lincoln

Your Daily RESET!

What areas of your life do you need to change perspective to appreciate the beauty?

Day 253

"Today what did I do for my mind? My body? My spirit? My relationships? My creativity and passion?"

~ Author Unknown

Your Daily RESET!

Ask yourself this question at the end of every day. What will you do today to invest in your future self?

Day 254

"Fears are stories we tell ourselves."

~ Laura Davis

Your Daily RESET!

Think back on times when you convinced yourself something was going to be more challenging or difficult than it actually was and fear held you back from acting when you should. What did you learn from the experience? How can you apply that learning to a situation in your life today?

Day 255

"You have the choice to make the rest of your life average...or extraordinary."

~ Dr. Jason Brooks

Your Daily RESET!

Which do you choose? Are you content living an average life or do you want something truly extraordinary? What could you be doing different today to live the life of your choice?

Day 256

> "Life doesn't always give you second chances, so take the first one."
>
> ~ Author Unknown

Your Daily RESET!

Think back on a time when you hoped for a second chance that never came. Maybe it was in a relationship where you wanted to say "I'm sorry!", but you never got the chance. The Law of Diminishing Intent says that the longer we wait to do something, the less likely it is that we will do it. If you feel God leading you in a particular direction, don't wait for a second chance...Do it!

Day 257

"God knows who belongs in your life and who doesn't. Trust and let go. Whoever is meant to be there, will still be there."

~ Author Unknown

Your Daily RESET!

Is there someone in your life today you know is not healthy for you to be around? Are there folks you should lovingly tell you just cannot spend time with anymore because it's not best for you or them? God may be prompting you to end relationships, with care, compassion, and confidence. Just something to think about.

Day 258

"What defines us is how well we rise after falling."

~ Lionel from *Maid in Manhatten*

Your Daily RESET!

Think back to a time when you were not successful with something you tried to do. How did that situation impact your future decisions to risk trying something new?

Day 259

"If we did all the things we were capable of doing we would literally astonish ourselves."

~ Thomas A. Edison

Your Daily RESET!

Think about a time when you did something you didn't believe you could do before you started. What did you learn about yourself through the experience? What situations are you facing today you that view as insurmountable where you need to apply that learning so you can achieve something truly extraordinary?

Day 260

"Allow yourself to be a beginner. No one starts off being excellent."

~ Author Unknown

Your Daily RESET!

Think about a time you were a "beginner". How did you grow through that experience? In what areas of your life are you facing similar situations for learning and growth today?

Day 261

"The price of anything is the amount of life you exchange for it."

~ Henry David Thoreau

Your Daily RESET!

What are you giving your life for today? Is the investment of your time and yourself worth it? Where do you need to change your focus in order to get the greatest value from your life?

Day 262

"When you fear your struggles, your struggles consume you. When you face your struggles, you overcome them."

~ Author Unknown

Your Daily RESET!

What are you struggling with today? How confident do you feel in your ability to face these struggles, one step at a time, and overcome them? Are you looking at the immensity of the problem overall or just the next step you need to take? Keep it simple and fear can't take hold.

Day 263

"It's time to start living the life you've only imagined."

~ Henry James

Your Daily RESET!

What's holding you back from living the life you've always imagined? What do you need to let go of that's standing in your way? What do you need to embrace about yourself that will move you down the road of living your purpose with passion?

Day 264

"You fall, you rise, you make mistakes, you live, you learn. You're human, not perfect. You've been hurt, but you're alive. Think of what a precious privilege it is to be alive-to breathe, to think, to enjoy, and to chase the things you love."

~ Author Unknown

Your Daily RESET!

Though we face challenges, we have the ability to rise and overcome. Think about a time when you overcame a challenging situation in your life. What did you learn from the experience you can apply to your life today?

Day 265

"Your mission: Be so busy loving your life that you have no time for hate, regret, or fear."

~ Karen Salmansohn

Your Daily RESET!

What role does hate, regret, and fear play in your life? Are they so prevalent that you have difficulty experiencing love for yourself and others? Make a commitment now to begin focusing on love and make it the center of your life.

Day 266

"We do not heal the past by dwelling there, we heal the past by living fully in the present."

~ Marianne Williamson

Your Daily RESET!

What do you need to let go of from your past to live fully free in the present?

Day 267

"One has to find a balance between what people need from you and what you need for yourself."

~ Jessye Norman

Your Daily RESET!

How balanced do you feel today between the expectations you have of yourself and the expectations others have of you? If you feel out of balance, what needs to change to be better for you? We can only be the best for others if we are able to be the best for ourselves.

Day 268

"I'm gonna make the rest of my life, the best of my life."

~ Author Unknown

Your Daily RESET!

Do you believe you have the ability to start a new course in your life today and make the rest of your life the best of your life? What do you need to let go of from the past that's holding you back? What do you need to take hold of today to create a better future. God has great things in store for you if you just let go and trust Him to lead.

Day 269

> "You can't reach for anything new if your hands are still full of yesterday's junk."
>
> ~ Louise Smith

Your Daily RESET!

How much of yesterday's challenges and failures do you carry with you today? What do you need to let go of in order to embrace the gifts today has to offer?

Day 270

"For I know the plans I have for you declares the Lord, Plans to Prosper you and not to harm you. Plans to give you a hope and a future."

Jeremiah 29:11, <u>The Holy Bible</u>

Your Daily RESET!

Do you know that God has a purpose for your life? Do you know what your purpose is?

Day 271

"In art and dream may you proceed with abandon. In life may you proceed with balance and stealth."

~ Patti Smith

Your Daily RESET!

How successful are you at balancing your dreams with your actions? Do you spend most of your time dreaming of the future? Do you spend most of your time working, working, working with no clear direction? For a life of success, we need balance in both.

Day 272

"At some point, you have to realize that some people can stay in your heart but not in your life."

~ Sandi Lynn

Your Daily RESET!

How difficult is it for you to release toxic people from your life? Is it easier to deal with the pain of the relationship rather than say "Goodbye"?

Day 273

"I can't tell you the key to success, but the key to failure is trying to please everyone."

~ Ed Sheeran

Your Daily RESET!

How important is pleasing everyone in your life? In what ways has this desire to please others held you back from living the life you have been called to live? Think about a time when you did something that wasn't popular with others even though you knew it was the right thing to do? What was the experience like? What did you learn from the experience?

Day 274

"Storms make trees take deeper roots."

~ Dolly Parton

Your Daily RESET!

What storm have you faced in your life that helped you to grow stronger? In whay ways did you grow through the experience? How can you use your experience to inspire others?

Day 275

"Don't carry your mistakes around with you. Instead, place them under your feet and use them as stepping stones!"

~ Author Unknown

Your Daily RESET!

What mistakes have you made that have been building blocks for your life? What mistakes do you need to make to continue to grow?

Day 276

"The difference between who you are and who you want to be is what you do."

~ Author Unknown

Your Daily RESET!

What are you doing today to become who you want to be in yourself, your relationships, your faith, your physical health, your mind, your work?

Day 277

"The only way to get better is to surround yourself with people who believe in you."

~ Author Unknown

Your Daily RESET!

Make a list of the 5 people you spend the majority of your time with. In what ways are you learning and growing from them?

Day 278

"Be thankful for friends who care about you."

~ Victoria Osteen

Your Daily RESET!

Make a list of your friends who you know without a doubt care deeply about you. Take a few minutes to send them a message or give them a call today to let them know how much you appreciate their friendship and how much they mean to you.

Day 279

"A heart of gratitude in the morning can transform the course of your entire day."

~ Edmund S. Lee

Your Daily RESET!

Take time now to make a list of the things you are thankful for. Carry this list with you today and as you go through the day, add to the list as you encounter people, situations, and things you're grateful for.

Day 280

"Whether you think you can, or think you can't, you're right."

~ Henry Ford

Your Daily RESET!

Which is most like you? Do you focus more on what you can do or what you can't? Don't let the limits on what you think be the limits of what you can achieve.

Day 281

> "So be strong and courageous! Do not be afraid and do not panic before them. For the Lord your God will personally go ahead of you. He will neither fail you nor abandon you."

Deuteronomy 31:6, *The Holy Bible* (NLT)

Your Daily RESET!

Think back on a time when you had to be strong and courageous in a challenging situation. Where did your strength come from to make it through? What did you learn about yourself? God is walking by your side to help you through any challenge you face. All you have to do is let go, trust in His leading, and follow His steps. He's waiting for you with open arms.

Day 282

"When we focus on the positive and give thanks in every season, amazing things will start to happen in our lives."

~ Dr. Jason Brooks

Your Daily RESET!

How often do you give thanks and focus on the positives in your life? Are you more of a "glass half empty" or "glass half full" type of person? Is an attitude of gratitude something that just seems out of reach for you? What's one thing you are thankful for today?

Day 283

"You can't go back from now to make a new start, but you can start now to make a new ending."

~ Dr. Jason Brooks

Your Daily RESET!

To what extent do the challenges of the past hold you back from living in the present and having hope for the future? What do you need to release from the past so you can focus on the future?

Day 284

"You are never too old to set another goal or to dream a new dream."

~ C.S. Lewis

Your Daily RESET!

What goals are you working to achieve today?

Day 285

"Without faith, hope, and trust, there is no promise for the future, and without a promising future, life has no direction, no meaning and no justification."

~ Adlin Sinclair

Your Daily RESET!

To what degree does faith, hope, and trust play a role in your life? Are you optimistic for the future or do you predominantly look at the negatives? Commit today to take your thoughts captive and when a negative thought enters, replace it with one of faith, hope, and trust.

Day 286

"When life changes to be harder, change yourself to be stronger."

~ Author Unknown

Your Daily RESET!

Think back on a time when you made it through a difficult situation or circumstance and realized, although painful, you grew as a result of the experience. Give thanks now for that season and the person you have grown to become as a result of the challenges you've faced through your life.

Day 287

"Often we are living our lives more as observers and passive participants rather than as confident, courageous, disciplined and intentional authors of our destiny."

~ Dr. Jason Brooks

Your Daily RESET!

Are you living your life with intentionality every moment of every day? Or, are you just going through the motions, floating through life at the whims of your circumstances or the expectations of others?

Day 288

"Accept what is, let go of what was, and have faith in what will be."

~ Sonia Ricotti

Your Daily RESET!

What do you need to let go of in your life? Pain? Guilt? Fear? Unforgiveness? Doubt? Make a list and commit today to starting the process to letting these thoughts, feelings, and baggage you've carried go.

Day 289

"To accomplish great things we just not only act, but also dream, not only plan, but also believe."

~ Anatole France

Your Daily RESET!

Make a list of the 10 most important things you want to accomplish in life. What steps are you taking today to help bring those things into reality?

Day 290

"Do one thing every day that scares you."

~ Eleanor Roosevelt

Your Daily RESET!

How often do you do something that scares you...something beyond what you thought you could do or accomplish? When we stretch ourselves, we grow. Look for opportunities today to do something that scares you and develops you into someone more than you were yesterday.

Day 291

"It's your road, and yours alone. Others may walk it with you, but no one can walk it for you."

~ Rumi

Your Daily RESET!

In what ways are you walking your road with confidence and courage?

Day 292

"There is no telling how many miles you will have to run while chasing a dream."

~ Author Unknown

Your Daily RESET!

What are you willing to sacrifice to bring your dreams to reality? What are you willing to give of yourself to live your purpose to the fullest? Make a list now of anything you are not willing to sacrifice to live the life you've always imagined.

Day 293

"You can't always wait for the perfect time. Sometimes, you have to dare to do it because life is too short to wonder what could have been."

~ Author Unknown

Your Daily RESET!

What have you been waiting to do? What's holding you back from doing it today?

Day 294

"The greatest gift you can give someone is your time. Because when you give your time, you are giving a portion of your life that you will never get back."

~ Author Unknown

Your Daily RESET!

List three people you need to reach out to today. Commit to making the connection and give the gift of your time.

Day 295

"The secret of change is to focus all of your energy, not on fighting the old, but on building the new."

~ Socrates

Your Daily RESET!

How easy is it for you to focus your attention to the opportunities of the future rather than on experiences of the past? What do you need to let go of today from your past so you can move forward with courage in creating an incredible future?

Day 296

"You have to fight through some bad days to earn the best days of your life."

~ Author Unknown

Your Daily RESET!

Think back on some difficult times in your life you overcame and persevered through. Maybe you are going through a season of challenge now. In what ways are you now growing through the experience. What strengths are you developing in yourself that will help equip you for the future?

Day 297

"No matter how many mistakes you make or how slow you progress, you are still way ahead of everyone who isn't trying."

~ Author Unknown

Your Daily RESET!

In what ways have you grown as a result of your mistakes?

Day 298

"Note to self. I am doing the best I can with what I have in this moment. And that is all I can expect of anyone, including me!"

~ Author Unknown

Your Daily RESET!

Take time now to answer the following question: Am I really doing the best I can do in all areas of my life? Am I giving my best to my marriage? My children? My friendships? My work? My physical health? My personal growth and development? My faith and spiritual life? Managing my money? If not, what areas need to change? Make a commitment to start the process today.

Day 299

"Stop hating yourself for what you aren't and start loving yourself for what you are."

~ Author Unknown

Your Daily RESET!

What self-limiting thoughts are you letting into your mind? When they creep in, immediately recognize and replace them with affirming thoughts to encourage and motivate yourself.

Day 300

"To be honest with you, I don't have the words to make you feel better, but I do have the arms to give you a hug, ears to listen to whatever you want to talk about, and I have a heart; a heart that's aching to see you smile again."

~ Author Unknown

Your Daily RESET!

Take time today to be aware of the needs of those around you. If someone needs a hug...give a hug. If someone needs an understanding ear...give them the gift of time and caring attention.

Day 301

"You will never change your life until you change something you do daily. The secret of your success is found in your daily routine."

~ John C. Maxwell

Your Daily RESET!

What is one thing you could do different today that would be better for you? Just one thing. Now...do it!

Day 302

"Man cannot discover new oceans unless he has the courage to lose sight of the shore."

~ Andre Gide

Your Daily RESET!

Think back on a time when you left the safety of a comfortable situation to embrace a new adventure. What did you learn about yourself through the experience? How did that experience influence who you are today?

Day 303

"I choose to be unstoppable. I am bigger than my concerns and worries. The strengths of others inspire me daily. I focus on my goal. I trust my intuition and live a courageous life."

~ Emily-Jane Elizabeth Veerman

Your Daily RESET!

What things are you worried or concerned about today? Where does your faith come from? What's keeping you going? Where are you putting your trust that tomorrow will be better than today? Don't give up on yourself or the vision of a better future ahead.

Day 304

"Whatever happened over this past year, be thankful for where it brought you. Where you are is where you're meant to be!"

~ Mandy Hale

Your Daily RESET!

Think back over the last year. Make a list of the challenges you faced? What did you learn from those experiences? In what ways have they made you stronger? Give thanks now for the challenges in life and the growth you've had as a result.

Day 305

"The future belongs to those who believe in the beauty of their dreams."

~ Eleanor Roosevelt

Your Daily RESET!

What are the dreams of your life? Are they clear in your mind? What is one thing you could do today to move in the direction of living your dreams?

Day 306

"You have to be real with yourself before you can be real with anyone else."

~ Author Unknown

Your Daily RESET!

When you look in the mirror, do you see the real you? Are you able to be honest with yourself about your feelings, your dreams, your purpose, your passion, your fears, and your successes. What areas of your life do you find it challenging to be honest with yourself about?

Day 307

"I do not fix problems. I fix my thinking. Then problems fix themselves."

~ Louise Hay

Your Daily RESET!

What are some thoughts you are keeping that are holding you back from being all you were created to be? In what ways do those thoughts need to change?

Day 308

"Take joy in how far you've come and have faith in how far you can go."

~ Dr. Jason Brooks

Your Daily RESET!

Take a moment to ponder the word "Joy"! What does joy mean to you? What areas of your life bring you joy? How intentional are you at focusing on joy and making it a part of your daily life. Joy is a choice...make the choice today to live in joy!

Day 309

"Every day is a new beginning, take a deep breath and start again."

~ Author Unknown

Your Daily RESET!

How difficult is it for you to let go of the baggage of yesterday and start new today? Start each day with a clean emotional slate and optimism for the day ahead.

Day 310

"Life is like a roller coaster. You can either scream every time there is a bump or you can throw your hands up and enjoy the ride."

~ Author Unknown

Your Daily RESET!

Do you find you're able to enjoy the ups and downs of life, knowing they're all part of the ride? What situations are you facing today that should be turned from fear to exhilaration?

Day 311

"I need to be startlingly clear. This thing of finding your authentic voice, expressing your blessed weirdness and revealing your soul isn't an elegant process. You don't do it to be cool. It's only real when it is ruthless, relentless and inevitable. But it is also a matter of personal and collective survival. Yes, it's that important. You are that critical."

~ Jacob Nordby

Your Daily RESET!

How difficult is it to be the real you? How often do you find yourself trying to meet the expectations of others rather than being true to yourself? What's one thing you could do different today to let the "real you" shine?

Day 312

"Be careful with your words. Once they are said, they can be only forgiven, not forgotten."

~ Hussein Nishah

Your Daily RESET!

Think back on a time when words you said hurt someone deeply. What did you learn from the experience? How intentional and concientious are you with the words you say?

Day 313

"Fall down seven times. Stand up eight"

~ Japanese Proverb

Your Daily RESET!

What are you facing today that's holding you down and you feel you can't recover from? What strength do you need to bring that will allow you to overcome and stand? Remember, you're stronger than you know and more resilient than you can imagine. With God holding your hand, all things are possible.

Day 314

"Don't let the noise of others' opinions drown out your own inner voice."

~ Steve Jobs

Your Daily RESET!

How often do other's opinions of you overshadow your inner voice and what you think and feel about yourself? How have these voices held you back from living the life God created you to live? How have you overcome the opinions of others in the past to move forward with pursuing your purpose and dreams?

Day 315

"Keep away from people who try to belittle your ambitions. Small people always do that, but the really great make you feel that you too, can become great. When you are seeking to bring big plans to fruition, it is important with whom you regularly associate."

~ Mark Twain

Your Daily RESET!

Think back to a time when someone belittled your dreams. What was that like? What do you remember from the experience? What did you learn about yourself that you can apply to situations today with folks who are not as supportive as you would like them to be, in decisions you're making, and directions you're taking you know are the right paths?

Day 316

"If you work really hard and are kind, amazing things will happen."

~ Conan O'Brien

Your Daily RESET!

Success comes through courage, commitment, connection, and contribution through work. All must be in place for true success to be achieved. Think back on a time when you were successful. What did you do to achieve success?

Day 317

"No one is in charge of your happiness except you."

~ Author Unknown

Your Daily RESET!

What's one thing you could do different today that would bring greater happiness into your life?

Day 318

"An arrow can only be shot by pulling it backward. When life is dragging you back with difficulties, it means it's going to launch you into something great. So just focus and keep aiming."

~ Author Unknown

Your Daily RESET!

Think about a time when you faced challenges in your life. In what ways did you grow through those challenges?

Day 319

"Live as if you were to die tomorrow.
Learn as if you were to live forever."

~ Mahatma Ghandi

Your Daily RESET!

In what ways are you investing in
yourself today?

Day 320

"Always accept and feel comfortable with your flaws, that way no one can ever use them against you."

~ Author Unknown

Your Daily RESET!

How often do you find yourself feeling down because someone shone a spotlight on your flaws? How difficult is it for you to accept and love yourself just the way you are?

Day 321

"Find someone who wants you as much as you want them."

~ Author Unknown

Your Daily RESET!

Think about the most fulfilling past and present relationships in your life. What made them meaningful and fulfilling? Relationships where both individuals aren't equally committed to creating the best relationship possible often lead to frustration, pain, and disappointment. You have the ability and responsibility to choose the relationships in your life. Choose wisely.

Day 322

"Some people feel the rain. Others just get wet."

~ Bob Marley

Your Daily RESET!

What type of person are you? Commit now that during the next season of spring showers you will take a walk in the rain. Feel the water on your face and skin. Walk through the puddles. Dance! Skip! Embrace the experience of feeling the rain.

Day 323

"The highest form of wisdom is kindness."

~ The Talmud

Your Daily RESET!

Think back on a time when you displayed kindness to a family member or friend. Now, think about a time when you showed kindness and compassion to a stranger. What was that like for you? Look for ways to show kindness and love toward others today.

"Dreams + Work = Success"

~ Author Unknown

Your Daily RESET!

What do you think about this formula? Do you have another formula you've found to work in your life. If so, share it at https://www.facebook.com/drjasontbrooks

Day 325

> "Perfectionism is the mother of procrastination."
>
> ~ Michael Hyatt

Your Daily RESET!

How much of a challenge is procrastination for you? Did you know often people procrastinate because they are afraid of making a mistake? So, instead of taking a risk and trying, they just wait. Is this a struggle you face? Break through the fear and realize mistakes are part of life and are necessary to grow. Don't put off something challenging for you any longer. Take the risk and fly!

Day 326

"To wish you were someone else is to waste the person you are."

~ Sven Goran Eriksson

Your Daily RESET!

We often spend so much time and mental energy comparing ourselves to others and wishing we were someone else. Take time right now to make a list of the attributes you love about yourself. Focus on these today.

Day 327

"Live in the sunshine, swim the sea, drink the wild air."

~ Ralph Waldo Emerson

Your Daily RESET!

Look out your window or, if you are outside, take a look around you right now. What do you see? Take a moment to celebrate and enjoy the beauty of creation.

Day 328

"I am in competition with no one. I run my own race. I have no desire to play the game of being better than anyone, in any way, shape, or form. I just aim to improve, to be better than I was before. That's me and I'm free."

~ Jenny G. Perry

Your Daily RESET!

Where do you experience competition in life? Competition can be good in sports to motivate and challenge us to stretch beyond ourselves. But, in the game of life, our only competition is ourselves. We are daily competing to live our full potential each and every minute. How are you challenging yourself today to be the best "you" that you can be?

Day 329

"Don't workout so you can love your body. Workout because you love your body. There is a difference."

~ Lauren Bersaglio

Your Daily RESET!

What's your motivation for caring for your body? Are you pleased with your progress? If not, what is one thing you could do different to help you move closer to your goals?

Day 330

"Until further notice. Celebrate everything."

~ Author Unknown

Your Daily RESET!

What are you doing to celebrate and give thanks today?

Day 331

"Today will never come again. Be a blessing. Be a friend. Encourage someone. Take time to care. Let your words heal, and not wound."

~ Author Unknown

Your Daily RESET!

What's one thing you could do to show someone you care about them today?

Day 332

"When a child gives you a gift, even if it is a rock they just picked up, exude gratitude. It might be the only thing they have to give, and they have chosen to give it to you."

~ Dean Jackson

Your Daily RESET!

Take time today to be thankful for every gift given to you by your kiddos. If your children are grown, call them and tell them "Thanks" for something they did for you when they were younger. If you don't yet have children, commit now you'll treasure every moment you are given with them if you are blessed to be called a "Mommy or Daddy".

Day 333

"Everything you want is on the other side of fear."

~ Jack Canfield

Your Daily RESET!

In what way has fear held you back in the past? How is fear holding you back today? 365 times in the Bible we are told "Do not be afraid." God knows fear is a very real challenge in all our lives and He encourages us to trust in Him and resist our fear. Whatever you're facing in your life, He's got it covered and is working all things together for your good.

Day 334

"Every time I thought I was being rejected from something good, I was actually being re-directed to something better."

~ Dr. Steve Maraboli

Your Daily RESET!

Think back on a time when something didn't happen the way you had hoped but later found it actually worked out better than you could have ever imagined. What did you learn from the experience? What did you learn about yourself from the experience? God has a perfect purpose and plan for your life. Seek Him and He will direct your steps.

Day 335

"Just because you fail once doesn't mean you're going to fail at everything. Keep trying and believe in yourself!"

~ Marilyn Monroe

Your Daily RESET!

What have you learned from your failures in life? How have they contributed to the person you are today? Remember, God can take the broken pieces of your life and make something beautiful.

Day 336

"It only takes one person to change your life...you!"

~ Ruth Casey

Your Daily RESET!

What do you need to change in your life today to be in a better place? What do you need to start doing differently that would allow you to live your dreams and touch other's lives?

Day 337

"Be positive, patient, and persistent."

~ Author Unknown

Your Daily RESET!

Take time now to make a list in answer to the following questions: In what areas of your life do you need to be more positive? In what areas of your life do you need to be more patient? In what areas of your life do you need to be more persistent?

Day 338

"You are free to choose, but you are not free to alter the consequences of your decisions."

~ Ezra Taft

Your Daily RESET!

There are consequences to everything in life. Some good…some bad. Think back on a time when the consequences of a decision you made were not what you expected. What have you learned about consequences in your life?

Day 339

"Don't be afraid to stand for what you believe in, even if it means standing alone."

~ Author Unknown

Your Daily RESET!

What are the beliefs in your life that are foundational to who you are? Where did your beliefs come from? Commit today to respect the rights of others to believe as they feel led but also stand firm on your own beliefs.

Day 340

"Inhale confidence. Exhale doubt and fear."

~ Amanda Mason

Your Daily RESET!

How confident are you in your abilities to face the challenges and opportunities of today? Do doubts in yourself hold you back from pushing forward and accepting new adventures? Every day you're learning and growing to become the person you were created to be.

Day 341

"There is no passion to be found in settling for a life that is less than the one you are capable of living."

~ Nelson Mandela

Your Daily RESET!

In what ways are you settling for a less than abundant life today?

Day 342

"Never settle. Fight for the life, the career, the dreams, the love that you deserve."

~ Mandy Hale

Your Daily RESET!

Complacency is the first step on the road to living an unfulfilled life. What do you need to be intentional about today that will move you forward to build the life you were created to live and unleash your full potential?

Day 343

"It takes as much energy to wish as it does to plan."

~ Eleanor Roosevelt

Your Daily RESET!

What are you wishing for in your life? Do you have a plan to support your wishes and dreams. If not, start to build your plan today.

Day 344

"A bird sitting on a tree is never afraid of the branch breaking, because her trust is not on the branch but on it's own wings. Always believe in yourself."

~ Author Unknown

Your Daily RESET!

What strengths have helped you become who you are today? Where are you putting your trust and faith? God has equipped you with everything you need to be successful as you walk with Him through the day.

Day 345

"Surround yourself with only people who are going to lift you higher."

~ Oprah Winfrey

Your Daily RESET!

How intentional are you about the people you allow into your life? Do you surround yourself with folks who encourage, inspire, and motivate you or those who criticize, chastise, and belittle your dreams? What choices do you need to make today about the people you're spending your time with?

Day 346

"The most important financial principle is contentment. It brings peace, not apathy."

~ Dave Ramsey

Your Daily RESET!

In what areas of your life are you content? In what areas are you not content? Do you spend the majority of your time focused on the things you don't have rather than those you do have? Take time now to give thanks for the blessings in your life.

Day 347

> "Insanity: doing the same thing over and over again and expecting different results."
>
> ~ Albert Einstein

Your Daily RESET!

In what ways are you modeling insanity in your life? What should you begin doing different today?

Day 348

"Happy are those who take life day by day, complain very little, and are thankful for the little things in life."

~ Author Unknown

Your Daily RESET!

What is frustrating you today? What's not working out for you the way you had hoped or planned? What's making you angry? Take time now to give thanks for those challenges knowing in each of those experiences, you are becoming stronger through the strife.

Day 349

"Life begins at the end of your comfort zone."

~ Neale Donald Walsch

Your Daily RESET!

Think about a time when you stretched beyond your comfort zone to do something that scared you. What was that like for you? What did you learn about yourself. What are you thinking of doing today that is beyond your comfort zone? Go for it!!

Day 350

"So many people walk around with a meaningless life. They seem half-asleep, even when they're busy doing things they think are important. This is because they're chasing the wrong things."

~ Mitch Albom

Your Daily RESET!

Do you find yourself just going through the motions of life, lacking meaning and focus? Do you go through each day with the same routine, almost sleep-walking through life? You were created for more! God has a purpose for your life and He's waiting for you to come to Him to discover your reason for living.

Day 351

"Never let the things you want make you forget the things you have."

~ Author Unknown

Your Daily RESET!

Take time today to make a list of the things you are thankful for in your life. Celebrate those things and give thanks to God for the blessings in your life.

Day 352

"Actions prove who someone is. Words prove who someone wants to be."

~ Author Unknown

Your Daily RESET!

Actions speak louder than words. What are your actions saying about who you are? Who would those closest to you say you are based on your actions?

Day 353

"I myself am made entirely of flaws, stitched together with good intentions."

~ Augusten Burroughs

Your Daily RESET!

How easy is it for you to be honest with yourself and your shortcomings, but see past those and celebrate the incredible person God created you to be? Make a list of the flaws that God has turned to strength in you to touch the lives of others.

Day 354

"When you knock on the door of opportunity do not be surprised that it is 'Work' who will answer."

~ Brendon Burchard

Your Daily RESET!

What are you working toward accomplishing today?

Day 355

> "Life will always try to make things difficult for you, but every time you overcome difficulties, you come out stronger."
>
> ~ Author Unknown

Your Daily RESET!

Think about a time when you overcame a challenging situation. What did you learn about yourself through the experience? In what ways did you grow? Take time now to give thanks for the challenges and the specific areas where you grew as a result.

Day 356

"When you focus on problems, you will have more problems. When you focus on possibilities you'll have more opportunities."

~ Author Unknown

Your Daily RESET!

Is it easier for you to think of the problems or possibilities in your life? Make a list of the possibilities you see today in your life and the opportunities ahead for you.

Day 357

"No one is 'too busy' in this world. It's all about priorities."

~ Author Unknown

Your Daily RESET!

How often do you use the excuse "I'm too busy to ...". Do you recognize it as an excuse? In reality, if something is a priority, you will find a way to get it done. Is there something in your life now you know you need to do but you've been using the excuse "I'm too busy"? Make a change today.

Day 358

"Success is like your own shadow. If you try to catch it you will never succeed. Ignore it and walk in your own way, and it will follow you."

~ Author Unknown

Your Daily RESET!

Take a few minutes to write your definition of success. What would you be doing, thinking, feeling, and saying to let you know you are successful? Having a crystal clear picture in your mind of what success looks like will help you recognize it when it comes.

Day 359

"The beauty of life is, while we can't undo what is done, we can see it, understand it, learn from it, and change."

~ Jennifer Edwards

Your Daily RESET!

Take time to write some of the things you've learned through your experiences in life? What have you learned about yourself? What have you learned about others? What different choices for change do you need to be making today based on the things you've learned through your life?

Day 360

"Just be yourself."

~ Author Unknown

Your Daily RESET!

On a scale of 1 to 10, how difficult is it for you to be yourself? Do you believe you are authentic or do you spend your time and effort trying to be what others want you to be. What's one thing you should start doing today to be more authentic? What's one thing you should stop doing today?

Day 361

"Happiness is not a matter of intensity but of balance and order and rhythm and harmony."

~ Thomas Merton

Your Daily RESET!

Think back on the times when you were happiest in your life. What were you doing? What were you experiencing? Were you overwhelmed and being pressured from all directions? Or, were you feeling balanced, focused, and intentional about who you are and what you were doing? Happiness is an emotional result of living a life on purpose with passion.

Day 362

"My soul is open. My heart is ready. My time is now."

~ Author Unknown

Your Daily RESET!

Are you open and willing to embrace the future that's ahead for you? Is there anything in you that's standing in the way? Do you trust God has great plans for you and His plans for your life are best?

Day 363

"Don't be pushed by your problems; be led by your dreams."

~ Ralph Waldo Emerson

Your Daily RESET!

Take time to make a list of your problems. Now, make a list of your dreams. Which of these lists is longer? Are you focused more on the problems in your life or your dreams and opportunities? Commit now to take time each day to read through your list of dreams and make those the focus of your life, not your problems.

Day 364

"If you did not care at all about what anyone else thought about you, what would you do differently, or change in your life?"

~ Brian Tracy

Your Daily RESET!

In what ways are the thoughts and expectations of others holding you back from living the life you've dreamed? What goals are you setting aside because they may not be popular or understood by others?

Day 365

"Never let the odds keep you from doing what you know in your heart you were meant to do."

~ H. Jackson Brown Jr.

Your Daily RESET!

Think about a time when you overcame significant obstacles to achieve something. What did you learn about yourself through that experience? How did the experience impact who you are today? Is it challenging, as you face new and bigger obstacles, to remember the times you were successful in the past and believe today you can be an overcomer again.

Your Daily RESET

Daily Inspiration and Motivation for Living Your Life of Purpose with Passion

RESET: Reformatting Your Purpose for Tomorrow's World

Dr. Jason Brooks

Imagine for a moment you are standing in front of an audience, looking out into the crowd at many faces. Their expressions are sad, sorrowful, and sympathetic. You realize quickly by scanning the room that you are giving a eulogy at a funeral. And, to your surprise, this funeral happens to be your own.

What will you say about your own life, your work, your relationships...your legacy?

What is the expression on your face? Are you sad and full of a sense of loss and regret—not because you've passed, but because you didn't live the life you imagined.

All of us, at some point, struggle with imbalance in our lives, our relationships, our faith, our personal growth, our finances and our careers. Maybe for you a RESET is critical. Or, maybe you've simply reached a point where you're just going through the motions of life without a clear sense of purpose or passion. Either way, this book will help.

Your RESET is waiting for you!

> Available online at Amazon.com, BN.com or from DrJasonBrooks.com

For more information on the ministry of Dr. Jason Brooks Outreach, and additional resources to help you live your life of purpose with passion, visit us today.

www.DrJasonBrooks.com

Connect via Social Media

You're invited to connect with Dr. Jason and the growing community of folks who are committed to living a life of purpose with passion. We're here to encourage, inspire, heal, learn and grow together. You are always welcome and we look forward to getting to know you and supporting you on your journey.

Facebook
www.facebook.com/drjasontbrooks

Twitter
www.twitter.com/drjasonbrooks

Instagram
www.instagram.com/drjasonbrooks

Linkedin
www.linkedin.com/in/jasontbrooks

Bestselling Author...
Inspirational Speaker...
Life Success Strategist...
Leadership Consultant...
Husband...Father...Friend!

Recognized as one of the most prominent emerging voices in personal and organizational transformation, Dr. Jason is also likely to be one of the most authentic, transparent, and "real". Seen by many as the "youth pastor" of personal change, growth, and success, his life mission of "bringing hope, healing, growth and inspiration to everyone he meets" provides the foundation and focus where his purpose and passion are fully unleashed.

As the bestselling author of *RESET: Reformatting Your Purpose for Tomorrow's World*, inspirational speaker, life and leader coach, and leadership development consultant, Dr. Jason brings a heart for helping others to achieve their greatest potential and success.

Dr. Jason has over 22 years experience in senior leadership and executive level roles in multi-million and multi-billion dollar Fortune 100 and Fortune 500 organizations in multiple industries including church and faith-based ministry, consulting, healthcare, hospitality, distribution, and manufacturing. He is an expert in leading personal and organizational transformation of all kinds.

While he has been blessed with incredible career success, his true heart's passion is in seeing lives changed by bringing hope, healing, and inspiration to people around the world and helping church, ministry, and business leaders maximize their potential. This has led Dr. Jason to create opportunities to touch individual lives as an author, speaker, coach and consultant and to bring change, growth, and success to churches, ministries, and secular organizations through speaking at events and seminars, executive coaching, and leadership development.

Dr. Jason is a passionate learner and teacher. He has earned the degrees of Doctor of Philosophy in psychology, Master of Science in mental health counseling, Master of Business Administration and Bachelor of Science in management. As a teacher, he has served as an adjunct faculty for multiple universities including Lipscomb University, Liberty University, and Trevecca University. He loves to take the opportunities for personal growth and development he has been given to pour into the lives of others.

In addition, he is a Certified Executive Coach, Board Certified Coach with specialty designations as a leadership coach, executive coach, business coach, corporate coach, and career coach. He is also a National Certified Counselor and a Board Certified Christian Counselor.

Dr. Jason lives just north of Nashville, Tennessee with his bride, Darla and three wonderful children, two sons and a daughter. Their daughter was adopted from China and came to her "Forever Family" at nine months old. He is actively involved in his church families at Long Hollow Baptist Church and Lifechurch.tv in multiple areas of purpose-focused, servant leadership.

His ministry of bringing hope, healing, growth, and inspiration to everyone he meets flows through him in every area of life and he finds no greater joy than seeing lives changed...one step at a time.

Trust in the Lord with all your heart, and do not depend on your own understanding. Seek His will in all you do, and He will show you which path to take.

Proverbs 3:5-6 (NLT)

ISBN 978-0-9909893-0-1

www.ingramcontent.com/pod-product-compliance
Lightning Source LLC
Chambersburg PA
CBHW031403290426
44110CB00011B/243